THE
WESTCHESTER
KIDS

Jacqueline Gutstein

CHAYA PUBLISHING

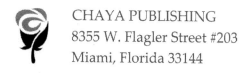 CHAYA PUBLISHING
8355 W. Flagler Street #203
Miami, Florida 33144

CHAYA PUBLISHING and colophon are
trademarks of CHAYA ROSE CORPORATION.

Published by: CHAYA PUBLISHING, Miami, Florida
Editor: Eve Arroyo, evearroyo.com

JacquelineGutstein.com
Inquiries: JacquelineGutstein@att.net

Library of Congress Control Number: 2021906047

ISBN: 978-1-7337203-2-8

First Edition

Printed in the United States of America

10 9 8 7 6 5 4 3 2 1

DEDICATION

To all the Westchester Kids who made living

in this small slice of South Florida so special

and to those who are no longer with us

including my brother

Max Gutstein, 1965 – 2018.

Jacqueline Gutstein with her Westchester Kid brother, Max,
who was fondly known as "Muscle" by a family friend.

AUTHOR'S NOTE

I wanted to compile this book with real-life stories and memories from the kids who lived and grew up in Westchester, an unincorporated four-square-mile neighborhood in South Florida, and hold this special town dear in their hearts.

There are many social media groups about Westchester with thousands of members that still share stories and old pictures from our neighborhood and reminisce about a bygone era.

Living and growing up in Westchester was truly life changing for all of us. My family moved there in the early 1960s from Little Havana, when life was simple, and you left the front door open all day to get the crosswind through the house. Only a screen door would protect you from the mosquitoes and unwanted stray animals.

It was a place where kids played outside from sunrise to dusk. Neighbors greeted one another, and children played in the streets and rode bicycles from block to block. You'd find chalk marks on the sidewalks from hopscotch games played earlier in the day, kids gliding on adjustable skates with metal wheels and clamps that grasped the front of their sneakers. It was a time when a stranger would knock on the door and ask to use the phone, and you'd let him or her in and offer them water or coffee, or the lady next door would stop by to borrow some sugar or milk. Fear was nonexistent, and strangers would become friends.

There were no cell phones or tablets to distract your attention, and only local television channels were available. The TVs that people owned were black and white—until color came along—with rabbit ear antennas, and you actually had to get up off the sofa to change the channel. It was a time where families sat down each evening at the kitchen table to eat their meals together and talk about things that had happened that day, either at work, school, or in the neighborhood.

There were so many families with children living in Westchester, making friends was easy. Now and then, neighbors invited you over for dinner when they were making your favorite meal. Many friendships made in Westchester remain today, some fifty-plus years later. Many of us see each other at school reunions or vacation together. Others stay connected via social media, even if they live in another state or country.

We're all older, some chubbier, some skinnier, some balder, but, hopefully, a little wiser. Many of the original Westchester Kids, who are mostly part of the baby boomer generation and Generation X, now have kids, grandkids, and great grandkids of their own. Some have lost their parents, siblings, spouses, extended family members, and classmates, but one thing we all have in common that no one can take from us, is our treasured memories.

Some of my friends still live in their Westchester homes, and although the white gravel roofs and terrazzo floors may have been replaced by sheet metal and ceramic tiles or hardwoods, the house they continue to live in holds lifelong memories of a special time.

I wanted to write this book to tell the story of this unique neighborhood, but I also knew it was the kids who lived and grew up in Westchester that could tell it best. I reached out to those I knew and many others from different social media sites regarding Westchester to contribute to this book, and the response I received was phenomenal.

I hope you enjoy all the stories contributed from thirty-one Westchester Kids, and that this book portrays how truly special this neighborhood was, and still is, in our hearts.

Note: The following real-life stories from the Westchester Kids are told from their respective recollections and memories.

Westchester

A small neighborhood in South Florida

that shaped the lives of so many families

Four-square-miles of homes, schools, stores, and innocence

hold so many memories seared into our souls

A kinship lives on in the Westchester Kids,

a bond so strong, one big family

Some have passed, some still live there,

and some have moved away,

But wherever we are, wherever we go,

Westchester owns a piece of our hearts.

— Jacqueline Gutstein

ACKNOWLEDGMENTS

My deep appreciation goes to all the Westchester Kids who contributed their stories and memories to make this book so special. I couldn't have done it without you.

A special thank you to my editor, Eve Arroyo, for her insight, talent, and guidance. Her input was invaluable to this project.

Much gratitude goes to, Aurora De Armas, who let me bounce ideas off her, and kept my fire burning to finish this book.

Finally, I want to give my sincere thanks to my parents, Margarita and the late Miron Gutstein, who made the decision to move to Westchester in 1966. I'll be forever grateful to you both for giving us three kids such a wonderful childhood in a safe and fun-filled neighborhood. And although my father passed away in 2017, and my younger brother Max less than a year later, I know they still watch over us. Living and growing up in Westchester shaped who I am today.

CONTENTS

1 | The Best Place in the Best of Times *Jeff Williams* 1

2 | Westchester Mall Was the Place to Be *Jonathan Brooks* 8

3 | Love at First Sight *Alex Maher* 13

4 | Best Years of my Life *Fran Watson* 20

5 | Number "7" *Tony Duque* 24

6 | The Shady Brew *Lee Goldwich* 31

7 | A Great Place to Live *Elizabeth Diaz Rizo* 36

8 | El Gringo de las Calles de "Wecheter" *Mike Moss* 44

9 | The Things We Got Away With *Rick Dronsky* 49

10 | Friends, Girls, Music, and Sports *Rafael A. Cubela* 54

11 | Remembering Eddie *Steve Moss* 59

12 | From Cuba to Westchester *Jacqueline Gutstein* 66

13 | A Wholesome Youth *Maria E. Garcia-Casals* 78

14 | A Special Place in My Heart *Evan Moss* 82

15 | Westchester Schools *Robin Lutes Brown-Cilliers* 87

16 | Baby Boomer Paradise *Debbie Dronsky Goldberg* 90

17 | The Good Ol' Days *Rhonda Beth Schwartzman Bandes*..........96

18 | Moving to "Nowhere" *Ann-Lynn Denker* 99

19 | Westchester Was Special *Vivian Sanchez-Villalba*................103

20 | Blue Light Special *Cristy Justo* 106

21 | The Best Place to Grow Up *Suzanne Schweitzer Shlian*........108

22 | New Home, New Life in Westchester *Martica D. Trueba* .. 112

23 | Part-Time Westchester Girl *Katherine M. Fuller* 119

24 | A Gringa in Westchester *Wendy Marie Welch* 123

25 | A Nerd No More *Irvin Lustig* 128

26 | For the Love of Teaching *Ruthann Paul-Suess* 131

27 | Westchester Girl at Heart *Lilymar Montenegro* 135

28 | Zayre: A Second Home *Donna Rose* 139

29 | Coming Full Circle *Gladys Velasco* 143

30 | My Buddy *Howard Shifke* 146

31 | Neighbors Are Extended Family *Pamela Ginsberg Reuter* .. 150

Epilogue ... Last Thoughts by Jacqueline Gutstein 153

1 | The Best Place in the Best of Times

The baseball player Lou Gehrig once famously said, "Today I consider myself the luckiest man on the face of the earth."

When I look back at my childhood growing up in Westchester in the '60s and '70s I also consider myself the luckiest man on the face of the earth.

I was so fortunate to grow up when I did. It was a time when, as kids, we had freedom coupled with responsibility. There were no cell phones, internet, GPS, etcetera to track our whereabouts. Our parents didn't always know where we were, but they always knew when we'd be home.

We rode our bikes everywhere as long as we got home before the streetlights came on. They never hovered over us, yet they expected my brother, sister, and me to fulfill our obligations. We went to bed when we wanted to, as long as we weren't late to school. I was expected to wake up on my own, make my breakfast, and get myself to school, and if I didn't, my older siblings would leave without me.

1

At an early age I learned about independence, responsibility, and accountability, lessons that have served me well in life. Imagine no cameras or social media to document all the stupid things we did as kids. If something happened to us, it was usually our fault, and we took care of it. We didn't cry about it, blame anyone else, or expect someone to make it go away. We owned it. It truly was the best of times to grow up in.

As influential on my development as the era I grew up in was, I believe *where* I grew up had an even bigger impact on me. I was born in 1961 and lived the first twenty years of my life in Westchester, on Twenty-First Street and Eighty-Fourth Avenue.

Westchester broke ground in 1955 as a post WWII development that offered affordable housing in a brand new suburb. Our neighborhood was at least seventy-five percent young families. Can you imagine growing up in a neighborhood where three out of every four houses had kids in them you knew? It was like hitting the playground lottery. If you wanted something to do, you just knocked on someone's door, and if they weren't home, you went to the next house. If we were playing a game where we were picking teams, we'd split up and canvas the neighborhood, and within ten minutes we'd have plenty of kids ready to play.

Back then we didn't have Chuck E. Cheese or Gymboree. We had playgrounds and the street in front of our house. If we wanted to play, we took the initiative ourselves to pick the games, organize, and referee them. If there were disagreements or fights, we resolved them ourselves. Again, these were the life lessons Westchester was teaching us. It really was idyllic.

But for me, Westchester was much more than a place to play, it was also a place to learn about different cultures, religions, and languages. I had the privilege of growing up with Cuban-American and Jewish-American families, some of the finest people I've ever met. The common denominators in most of these Westchester families were that they were intact, hardworking, and faith-based. Also, it was quite common for the grandparents to be living with or near their families.

When I grew up in Westchester it was truly a community bound by families, schools, and places of worship. This is the foundation I was brought up on, have lived by, and have passed on to my children. As much as society has changed, mainly because of technology, the foundation I learned in Westchester has not. I really do feel like the luckiest man on the face of the earth.

Sports in Westchester

From my earliest recollections, I always played sports. Starting in my backyard with my brother, Mark, to Little League, to high school, then on to the professional level, sports has always been a huge part of my life. Westchester provided the support and facilities for my development in whatever sport I was playing or learning.

My first love was baseball, and in 1969, when I was eight years old, I joined my first organized team, for Guaranty Bank in the Khoury League that played at the old Tropical Park on Bird Road. Back then, the park only had four diamonds, and wasn't big enough for the growing demands of so many boys and girls in Westchester playing baseball and softball. The following year, Tamiami Park on Coral Way opened with eight baseball diamonds, four softball fields, a pool, tennis courts, and enough room for expansion. I played seven more seasons of baseball at Tamiami Park, including two seasons where my father coached the team, a tradition I followed with my son's teams in Tampa.

I also played a few seasons of football for Westchester Optimist. The Colts, if I recall correctly. We practiced at Flagami Park on Coral Way and played our home games at Coral Estates Park on Ninety-Seventh Avenue. I was so small I'd do my game day weigh-ins with all my equipment on and still be under the weight limit by fifteen pounds. That's why I only played a few seasons.

I learned how to play basketball at the Young Men's and Young Women's Hebrew Association (YM-YWHA) on Eighth Street. Even though I wasn't Jewish, I had friends who were members there and they'd bring me in to play and learn on their courts. I went on to play on the basketball team for the West Miami Junior High Falcons for the three years I was there.

I learned how to swim at the Venetian pool and learned to play tennis at Salvador Park. Both facilities were in Coral Gables, on the outskirts of Westchester, but close enough for me to ride my bike to, which I often did. I also played on the tennis team for three years at West Miami Junior High, and then three more years at Miami Coral Park Senior High School. The Tamiami tennis courts served as our home venue for Coral Park's tennis team, so once again, I was playing at the same park where I spent so much time playing baseball.

While in my junior year in high school, I was introduced to a sport by my brother that would take my life in a different direction for the next twenty years, jai alai. I started by throwing a tennis ball with a cesta, a curved basket used to catch and throw the ball, behind the Westchester Movie Theatre, which had an enormous wall with a fence behind it. I later went from tennis balls to hard rubber balls, which made a loud thump. This was ideal for me, but not so much for the patrons of the theater trying to watch a movie. When I was "encouraged" to leave the premises, I'd go down to the shopping center behind the Western Auto store where they had a smaller sized wall, but no fence behind it, so if the ball got by me, it was a long run to get it. Also, the wall was only half the height of the theater wall, and I was just learning, so it wasn't uncommon for me to have to climb on the roof to collect all the misthrows.

I played jai alai behind the Westchester Shopping Center in my spare time between school, played on the tennis team, and had my job delivering the Miami Herald newspaper seven days a week starting at 5:00 a.m.

After I graduated from high school, I went to Miami Dade Community College South (now known as Miami Dade College) and also took a job at Miami Jai-Alai, where I could practice on the big court with a hard ball three times a week. Within a year, I was able to play with some of the Miami pros, which really elevated my game.

In May of 1982, I graduated from college and was accepted to Florida State University (FSU). I also signed my first professional contract to play at Big Bend Jai-Alai in Quincy, Florida, thirty miles west of Tallahassee. I was going to FSU during the day and playing professional jai alai at night; I was living the dream.

I graduated from FSU in 1984 and ended up playing fourteen seasons of professional jai alai in Ocala, and my last ten seasons in Tampa, retiring in 1998. It was a great run and provided a wonderful life for my family and me.

Jeff Williams when he played professional jai alai.

My high school alma mater produced some exceptional athletes in different sports, many going on to the pros. There were multiple baseball players who made it to the major leagues, including the Canseco brothers, Jose and Ozzie. After high school, Barry Smith became an All-American wide receiver at FSU and then went on to play in the NFL for the Green Bay Packers and Tampa Bay Buccaneers. Miami Coral Park also produced eight professional jai alai players including myself, my brother Mark, and Kent Getsee, who was my doubles partner on the tennis team.

Our high school didn't have a jai alai program or club, so I'm not sure why so many players came out of our school, more than any other high school anywhere in the United States. I only know that it all started for me behind the Westchester Shopping Center.

Jeff Williams

2 | Westchester Mall Was the Place to Be

While growing up in Westchester, the malls on both sides of Coral Way were the hot spots for everything from eating and shopping to entertainment for the young and old alike.

Think about the original Publix with their neon art deco sign, the department store Zayre offering popcorn as you shopped, and JByrons the place to be for your back to school wardrobe.

My first memories of the Westchester Mall are of Lionel Playworld, where most of my toys and bicycles growing up were from. And who could forget their infamous kangaroo logo and that they were open twenty-four hours a day during the holidays, at a time when no one had those hours?

My most vivid early memory is when I stayed home sick from school and rummaged through the house and found a Santa list with corresponding Christmas gifts. My dismayed mother then took advantage of the Playworld holiday hours and exchanged all of the toys in the middle of the night to keep my belief in the jolly fat man alive.

By the time I entered Rockway Junior High School, the mall was becoming an even bigger focus in all of our lives. I certainly lucked out, because my BFF's family

Jonathan Brooks with his elementary school project in 1974.

owned the Bresler's 33 Flavors ice cream parlor, and that led to many after school walks home being redirected to the mall first. Much fun and many scoops were had at the sweet shop, that included days dressed as clowns to drum up business.

My favorite store was Hit Parade, the record store that had the best assortment of 45s, twelve-inch LPs, and posters. I remember getting the famous Farrah Fawcett swimsuit poster from her Charlie's Angels heyday there. They always had lists of the biggest music hits of the week and the most popular albums of the month. Musique's "In the Bush," Patrick Hernandez's "Born to be Alive," John Paul Young's "Love is in the Air," Ami Stewart's "Knock on Wood," Village People's "Y.M.C.A.," and Gloria Gaynor's "I Will Survive" were all gems taken home from the musical wonderland.

The mall had diverse shopping and business choices. They had karate, ballet, a pinball arcade, the pet shop Animal Lovers West, and a laundromat. There was also an incredible history for some of these businesses: Mister Donut before Duncan Donuts, Woolworth before Eckerd Drugs then Walgreens, and U-tote-M before 7-Eleven.

The selection of restaurants was also out of this world, even before the addition of our first Burger King, which was a must for many high school lunch breaks in order to get a free paper crown. There was Lum's that was known for their beer steamed hotdogs and take home beverage glasses, free with purchase. Lila's Restaurant had great lunch specials and was famous for their Cuban steak covered in shoestring fries way before there was a Rio Crystal. And I fondly remember ordering a big Sicilian pizza slice or two New York thin slices of pizza at Snack Shack, which I devoured while putting one on top of the other like John Travolta in *Saturday Night Fever*.

Another well-known eatery was Westward Ho! It was particularly popular for being the place to get a root beer or a steak before catching a matinee at the Loews Movie Theatre, a cinema I will never forget because I saw so many of the classics there. I saw *Airplane, Porky's, Grease, Blazing Saddles, Body Heat, Apocalypse Now, Star Wars*, and some of the best of the best of the numerous other vintage motion pictures of the time.

A handful of the other locales in the mall live on in my mind because they dealt with the many special occasions of life. There was the tuxedo rental shop everyone in the neighborhood used for formal events, proms, and weddings. The Hallmark store was a constant must for birthdays, get well wishes, congratulations, and anniversaries. And the flower shop kiosk in the middle of the mall, run by the beautiful brunette twins Toni and Terri, was a regular stop for fresh blossoms for Mom or a friend.

There are a few more spots I also need to mention on my trip down memory lane, as they hold special places in my heart. The Thom McAn shoe store, which got us through the Hush Puppies fashion phase. The ladies boutique Stuarts, which was the go-to store for my shopping loving friend. And Tico Fashions, the bargain priced clothing shop that was the place of my little sister's first job.

I must also point out that the memories of these places wouldn't have been possible had they not been used as the destinations for me as I was learning to drive. Many a trip was made then, using the backstreets to these locations, which were actually only ten blocks away from our home.

I think back now to how adultlike it felt, as I avoided the main roads of Eighty-Seventh Avenue and Coral Way. Sometimes I parked on the street by the fence that surrounded the mall's back parking lot, then squeezed through the barrier to access the back entrance of the mall, which was more convenient.

The Westchester Mall will always hold a sacred place in my heart for all of the fun adventures I had there. In my mind, and in the minds of many others, I believe the Westchester Mall was, and will always be, the place to be.

Jonathan Brooks

3 | Love at First Sight

I was about four years old when our family moved from the northeast side of Miami to the Westchester area. We had a nice corner lot with a big back yard. The front yard had a nice large grassy area where we played all kinds of sports. My brother, sister, and I attended Banyan Elementary School and later, Rockway Junior High School and then Miami Coral Park Senior High.

I can remember a couple of blocks away, on the corner of Coral Way and Eighty-Fourth Avenue, there was a large vacant lot I'd explore, looking for small burrowing owls. On the other end of the lot, there was a Publix, JByrons and a Walgreens. Walgreens still had the restaurant with stools and the long countertop that seemed to go on forever.

Eventually, that empty lot turned into a Kmart, Food Fair grocery store and a mall. That mall became our hangout and playground. A few of us neighborhood kids would play hide and seek in the mall area, running in and out of stores and hiding behind clothes racks and even sometimes in storage areas.

One of our favorite hiding places was in JByrons, which had a large entrance into the mall. Hiding places were endless and we were never kicked out. I got my first job at the little pet shop in the mall and my older sister worked at the Snack Shack. My brother worked as a busboy at the Westward Ho!, which was in the shopping center north of Coral Way, across from Kmart and near Lionel Playworld, which, to a little kid, was the most amazing place to visit.

On the rare occasions our family when out to eat, we enjoyed dining at Westward Ho!, Lum's, or Lila's Restaurant. I fondly remember going to Saturday matinees at the Westchester Theatre which was located in the corner of the shopping center where Playworld was.

Across from Publix, on Eighty-Seventh Avenue, was a small convenience store called U-tote-M where we'd usually stop in after school for sodas and snacks. Another staple in Westchester was Mister Donut located directly across the street from Burger King. Our neighbor worked there, and on occasion, would bring us a dozen doughnuts.

On the northwest side of Coral Way and Eighty-Seventh Avenue was another shopping center with Zayre department store as the anchor. Close to Zayre was a small store called Eagle Family Discount, which is where I worked during high school.

My brother Johnny was a year ahead of me, so I usually road in his car with him to school. Back then, there was a dirt lot that we parked in which we called the "Dust Bowl," and on rainy days, it turned into a large lake.

My brother and his friends all had monster trucks and we'd spend weekends going to Virginia Beach, which was the only beach that allowed vehicles on the sand. I thought I was the cool eleventh grader hanging out with a bunch of seniors, but I remember being upset and jealous when I saw them all board the buses to go to Grad Night.

Alex Maher with friends Maria E. Garcia-Casals and Jacqueline Gutstein hanging out at Virginia Key Beach.

I'm so grateful to have lived and grown up in Westchester and these memories are still in my heart and bring a smile to my face all these years later.

Meeting Maria

In eleventh grade at Miami Coral Park Senior High School, I took advanced art classes, and the majority of my art friends were seniors. We had many adventures visiting galleries and museums, and I even went on a trip to Europe with my two art teachers, Tom Wyroba and Ivy Edmunds.

In my senior year, I was also able to attend Robert Morgan Vocational Technical Institute, now the Robert Morgan Educational Center & Technical College. I spent three class periods at Miami Coral Park, took an early lunch, then got on a bus for the half hour ride to Robert Morgan, spending the rest of the day in a commercial and advertising art class there.

One day early in the school year at Miami Coral Park, I was walking through the halls when I saw *her*. She had big green eyes with long, shiny black hair. I remember thinking to myself, "there she is . . . the girl of my dreams." She was the kind of girl I'd like to marry someday.

As much as I was taken aback by her, I knew there was no way I would ever have a chance of meeting her. I was a shy, introverted, artistic nerd who wore T-shirts and old jeans to school. She dressed very nicely with high heels and wore makeup, and I assumed she was probably dating the captain of the football team. To be honest, Miami Coral Park had many beautiful girls, but there was something different about her.

Up until that point, I'd never believed in love at first sight. As luck would have it, she also was attending Robert Morgan, so I would see her at lunch and on the bus when she wasn't hitching a ride with one of her friends.

I remember searching my yearbook to find out what her name was. When I found her picture, I wasn't surprised to see it was Maria. It seemed like every other girl in my high school had that name. As the days passed, I'd see her in the school halls and try to get up the courage to speak with her, but my extreme shyness prevented me from doing so. One day on the bus ride home, I was sitting in front of Maria's best friend, Loretta. Maria took a different bus home, so I got up the nerve to say hello to her friend. I thought maybe that was the best way of finding out more about Maria and it turned out she did indeed have a boyfriend. My heart sank, but I wasn't surprised. The good thing was he didn't attend our high school.

In one of my art classes, I had an assignment to find a photograph of a person's face and draw it with pencil. I immediately thought about drawing Maria but had no idea how I would go about getting a photo of her. On my bus ride home one day, I mentioned to Loretta about my assignment, and that I really thought her friend with the green eyes was attractive and I'd like to draw her. Although she gave me an odd look, she said she'd ask Maria for a photo for my assignment.

Several days passed with no picture, so even though I didn't want to sound pushy, I finally asked Loretta if she was able to get one. She said that Maria told her that if I wanted it, I'd have to ask her myself. I was doomed! What would she think of a stranger coming up to her and asking for a portrait?

Believe me, I tried, but I couldn't muster up the nerve to ask at that time. What made matters even worse was that Loretta pointed me out to her in the halls, so she knew what I looked like. I didn't have much self-confidence back then, so I believed Maria wouldn't give me the time of day.

It just so happened that one day, I was late for lunch and as I walked the empty hallways toward the cafeteria, I noticed someone rounding the corner and coming straight at me. It was my dream girl, Maria! I nervously looked around for a door to step into, but before I knew it, she was standing right in front of me. Through my nervousness, I was able to ask her for a photo. She mentioned to me that she'd just taken some modeling pictures and she'd bring a proof sheet for me to choose the one I wanted to draw.

A day or so later, she showed me a contact sheet with many head shots to choose from. I thought they all looked beautiful, but I finally narrowed it down to one. A few days later she brought me an eight-by-ten-inch head shot and now the pressure was on me to create a drawing that would impress her.

From then on, Maria and I always had lunch together and sat next to each other on the bus ride to Robert Morgan. I remember thinking, after I only knew her for about a week, that she was the girl I wanted to marry and spend the rest of my life with.

Our first real date was to our Homecoming dance. I nervously asked her one day at school and she accepted. Then, the next day, she came to me and said she had an issue. I think my heart stopped but was quickly relieved when she said her mom would have to chaperone us to the dance. Knowing she was brought up in a traditional Cuban household, I wasn't surprised at all, and the chaperoning continued all our dating years.

Sometime during my senior year, I wasn't sure what I was going to do after high school, so I decided to join the U.S. Navy. After boot camp, I came home on leave, and we decided to get married. Maria planned the entire wedding while I was deployed on a ship for six months.

When I returned, I flew home and got hitched with my high school sweetheart! That was in August of 1981 and we've been happily married ever since!

Alex Maher

Maria and Alex, high school sweethearts in 1980.

*Maria and Alex Maher have been
happily married since 1981.*

4 | Best Years of my Life

I was so blessed to live in Westchester from the time I was two years old until I was twenty-two and honestly, those were the best twenty years of my life. I thank God every day for my childhood and school years at Everglades Elementary, West Miami Junior High, and Miami Coral Park Senior High. It was full of sports, after school activities, lots of good laughter, and fun-filled times with friends and neighbors.

My brother Michael (five years older), Jackie (four years older) and Greg (two years younger) also experienced the same happy life growing up in Westchester with the best parents on earth, Jack and Uca, who have been happily married for sixty-six years and are still healthy at ninety-one and ninety-two years old respectively. I have countless memories as a kid, of riding my bike fast through the Westchester Shopping Center when the carnival was there and trying not to run people over.

I enjoyed driving to Tropical Park in my red 1970 Toyota Corolla and beating some friends in tennis. But what I loved the most was training and running with Mitch Moses from Eighty-Second Avenue, down Sixteenth

Street, over to Ninety-Seventh Avenue, up to Coral Way and back to Eighty-Second Avenue. We called that "the loop." Mitch was a huge motivator and always supported me in every sport I played.

My dear friend Jose "Choco" Barraza and I would drive around the neighborhood at night blasting those awesome '70s tunes from my car speakers and probably annoying the neighbors. One of the funniest times I remember was attending a pep rally and watching Juan Amador show off his athletic talents. That's where he got his nickname "Perro Caliente" (hot dog). My scariest moment while living in Westchester was risking my life accepting a dare to walk over the street traffic, *on top of* the fenced-in catwalk, not inside, spanning the SR 826 off-ramp from West Miami Junior High to my house on Eighty-Second Place.

My fondest memories of all-time are of my BFF, Mary Fahmie, may she rest in peace. We rode bikes to Coconut Grove and Crandon Park beach almost every weekend, played together on the softball and volleyball teams as well as cheerleading. We hung out every single day from fifth grade to twelfth grade. Many times, I even helped clean her house where she lived with her eight brothers and sisters so she could come out and play.

At Miami Coral Park High there were three coaches that had the most influence on me, providing me with life lessons which I've carried with me throughout my entire adult life. Fran King was my volleyball coach who taught me that hard work and not giving up are critical because women athletes have the same opportunities as men athletes to achieve success in the sports world and in life in general.

Doug Wyckoff was my tennis coach. He taught me that setting high goals and being an overachiever was what you needed to become a world-class athlete in the sports arena or a world-class citizen on the world stage.

Gene Stage was my basketball coach and I learned the importance of competition, discipline, perseverance, and visualization while achieving my goals. He also taught me that if the team works, then the dream works.

These are learning lessons from my coaches that I apply in my life and share with my family, children, and grandchildren. Every day, I try to achieve something of greatness, brightness, or make a difference in somebody's life.

We Westchester Kids feel very fortunate that we grew up in a happy, healthy, safe and secure neighborhood where everyone watched out for each other. The people in our hood were good down-to-earth folks, where kindness and respect for each other was the norm and the front door to your home was unlocked every day you came home from school.

My biggest hope is that we preserve this type of upbringing for our children, grandchildren, and great-grandchildren, where their innocence, morals, and dreams are preserved. Where they can be raised organically in a warm and safe world and can indulge in nature, hike outdoors, climb trees, ride bikes, play ball, swim at the beach, and live their lives to their fullest, free of hatred, anger, and fear.

Let's share that Westchester "luv" and wholesomeness back into everyone's home and heart like we had. That's always been my biggest wish and prayer for everyone's life I've touched along my journey while growing up and living in the best part of Miami—Westchester.

Fran Watson

Fran Watson still resides in South Florida.

5 | Number "7"

After growing up in the suburb of Westchester, I've lived in two big cities, Chicago and Seattle. While I love having many conveniences within walking distance as an adult, the kid in me feels fortunate to have grown up in Westchester. I'm grateful for the number of fields of freshly cut grass where a kid could play sports and have wide-open spaces to have fun and explore. A young me would have missed out on a lot had I grown up in the concrete jungle of a metropolitan area.

My neighborhood in Westchester had wide "county strips," as we called them. They were the swath of grass between the street and everyone's front yard. When there weren't any cars parked on them, on our street, the other kids and I were able to make a big football field that went all the way to the sidewalk, with a neighbor's yard marking the out of bounds area. We played many other games on the street/county strip combination including stickball using a tennis ball instead of a rubber ball.

Although I lived in a demographic with a lot of baseball talent, two doors down, my best friends played Little League tackle football every year. When they weren't off at practice or a game, we played on our street. I began liking sports a lot at that point, and with the only Florida professional team being the Miami Dolphins who were usually in the playoffs and winning Super Bowls back then, football became my number one sport as both a fan and a player.

Looking back on those days, I realize that most of the fun activities I was able to do as a kid wouldn't have happened had I lived anywhere else. A bunch of things transpired like in the old cartoon of Mr. Magoo, where a blind old man nearly walks or drives into disasters when something coincidental happens, like an iron beam from a construction site appears and he steps on it at the right moment. Many things came together coincidentally for me to end up playing quarterback for our high school football team, which was something I'd never given any thought to until the day it happened, and I became a starter.

My passion for football started on my birthday around the age of ten when I received a brand new football, along with a book by the National Football League as a present. The book was fairly comprehensive, and it covered many aspects of the game such as the history, the rules, and instruction on how to play the game properly. It had chapters on passing, blocking, tackling, kicking, and even a paragraph about punting a football.

After reading that chapter, I went out with my new football to practice what I'd just read. I learned the ball should be dropped carefully to keep it level as it falls. It's important to make contact with the fat part of the ball, slightly to the left of the center line, so it can roll off the foot to the right, making the ball spiral in the air. This allows it to travel higher and farther than a wobbly ball would. Aerodynamics makes this possible. A punted ball should have the same spiral as when a quarterback throws a pass.

One day at Everglades Elementary School, our physical education coach Mr. Bringas was talking to us about football and asked me to demonstrate how to punt. I guessed he'd been watching me practice with the footballs they gave us to play with. I hit a beautiful spiral that went very high, and everyone said, "Ah." I was so flattered that our coach had chosen me to demonstrate and happy I was able to kick it well when I needed to. That experience stuck with me, giving me the confidence to do it later on when I tried out for the football team.

In elementary and junior high school, I had another friend who lived a few blocks away that I spent many hours hanging out in the woods at the end of his street. One of the fun activities we engaged in in those woods was throwing the cones from a pine tree that were the size of a plum or a peach. They made excellent projectiles.

On the other side of the forest was the back of a gas station and we grabbed some junk from their dumpster to use as targets. We had a tire and empty oil cans that we threw our missiles toward, and we made up games to see who could do it the best until the pine cones ran out. All that target practice over a couple of seasons allowed me to develop my throwing accuracy.

One day, the older of my two football playing friends said colleges were recruiting him as a senior in high school, and I should try out for tackle football. He thought I should get a year of experience before I went to the senior high school where he was playing and would be a first-team All-City player his senior year.

He told me I played well, and if I could play well in high school, colleges might give me a scholarship to play football. He offered to talk to my dad and explain it. He did, and from his chair with a beverage in hand, my dad said, "Okay sure."

I tried out for receiver and cornerback, but the other boys had been playing for a number of years already and were good ... too good. I didn't win any starting positions on the team, with the exception of punter, which I won easily.

We were a terrible team with zero wins about halfway through the season. I think we played eight or ten games. I'd always show up to practice about a half hour early with my football to practice my punting. After a few people got there, I'd stop, because the other boys would want to throw the football around and play catch.

One day, with about four or five games to go, one of the other guys and the head coach came up to me. The coach said, "Number seventy-five here thinks you can throw the football pretty well. Let me see you throw one." I motioned for someone to run, and I threw it in such a way he didn't have to break full stride; it was right on the money.

Then the coach said, "Do you want to play QB?" I was surprised it was even possible; it hadn't ever occurred to me to play the quarterback position, but I said, "Okay sure." I answered just like my dad had when I asked him if I could play football. I was a chip off the old block, and the next year as a tenth grader during tryouts for the JV team, I won the quarterback job.

My junior year I was the punter and backup to the senior quarterback and my senior year I started at both QB and punter positions. That never would have happened anywhere else but in Westchester, with all that space to play at that time, with those friends, and with that NFL book I was gifted that taught me how to punt a football.

Photo credit: Miami Coral Park Sr. High Yearbook Photographer

Tony Duque, number 7, punts the football at a high school game in 1978.

My Westchester Playground

I traveled back home to Westchester during Christmas many times to visit my mom. One year as I drove through my old neighborhood, I got the same feeling Chrissy Hynde must have had when she wrote the song "My City Was Gone." Everything was gone when she went back, but in my case, it was my playgrounds.

I was so saddened to see the expansive grass fields of Everglades Elementary School paved over with a building and portable classrooms. Where were those kids going to learn how to punt, or play football, softball, and soccer? It was not just the well-tended grass fields, it seemed like all the places I treasured were now only parking spaces.

When I was growing up, one of my favorite places was a thick forest near my house which is literally a parking lot now. Back then, some of my friends in the neighborhood and I made a clearing in the middle of the forest to have a place to hang out. There were two forests I played in. Only if you saw someone go into what I'll call, the Thick Forest, would you notice there was a thin trail, with some winding turns that went all the way from the road to our clearing. You could ride your bike all the way to it.

As construction occurred around us, we grabbed materials they threw out and put up a fort-like structure that had a leaky roof. We even had furniture. Our favorite piece was a huge empty wooden spool used for holding wiring we found that made a great coffee table. Old, discarded car bench seats we happened upon became our couches. We'd hang out in our fort all the way through senior high school. There was another smaller and much less dense area that I'll call the MotoCross Forest near another friend's house a few blocks away. One year while in junior high, he and his brother got matching Honda XR-75s motocross motorcycles, and the two boys made a circuit through that wooded area. I got plenty of turns to ride and made jumps over a big mound while we pretended we were Evel Knievel, the famous stunt performer.

The map below gives a good picture of how things have changed for today's kids who, unfortunately, don't have as much room to play as I did. I lived in the house that is circled, and around the corner, we always played football at the end of the block. Any time after school you could see six to ten kids playing touch football or baseball with a tennis ball so we didn't break any windows. How I miss those days and those times. That was my Westchester playground . . . the area where we Westchester Kids could just be kids and play.

Tony Duque

6 | The Shady Brew

I thought about all the places in Westchester I experienced growing up including the YM-YWHA on the corner of SW Eighth Street and Eighty-Sixth Court. I went to kindergarten there, attended summer sports camp, and played softball, basketball, and tennis there. My dad was always a coach; I wish he were still around to coach me.

My family went to the club's pool on the weekends, and my friends and I would occasionally sneak into vacant cabanas to hang out after school. I remember the switchboard operator at the front entrance, with the old telephone system and all those wires. We went in through the front entrance with our parents, but with our friends, we crawled under the fence. Almost everyone I knew went there.

Of all the schools I went to in Westchester, Everglades Elementary, West Miami Junior High, Rockway Junior High, and Miami Coral Park Senior High, most of my memories and friendships were made at Everglades. I don't remember all of my teachers, but I do remember my first grade teacher, who'd pull everyone who misbehaved by their ear, and my sixth grade teacher, who was my all-time favorite. She was a Miami Dolphins fan and once rewarded the entire class with bubble gum after I won a bet with her that quarterback Bob Griese would return from an ankle injury before the end of the 1972 season. Fortunately, I managed to avoid the "mean" teachers, except for the ear-puller. I also enjoyed the family spaghetti dinner fundraisers we had.

My brothers, friends, and I spent countless hours roaming the stores and sidewalks of the neighborhood shopping centers, particularly Lionel Playworld, and the pinball arcade at the Zayre department store. Sometimes, when we were bored, we'd throw shaved ice at unsuspecting shoppers in the grocery store. Sometimes we would move other kids' bikes from the front of Eckerd Drugs or Lionel Playworld to the other end of the shopping center. Imagine their surprise when they came out of the store to find their bike had mysteriously moved. Some weren't too happy, and I remember being chased through the parking lot on more than one occasion.

That center had plenty of places I remember like the movie theater where I saw *Grease* for the first time, the Carousel Salon where my mom got her hair done every weekend, the drug store where we once "borrowed" a chunk of chewing tobacco (no one told us you weren't supposed to swallow it; that's a mistake you only make once). Then there was the Air Force Recruitment Center, located down a narrow hallway I happened to peek into as I was walking by one day in 1979. I still remember the recruiter, standing there in his uniform in the middle of the office, looking straight out the door at the exact moment I happened to look in. He was quite the talker, and a few months later I was at Lackland Air Force Base in San Antonio, Texas, going through basic training.

We spent a lot of time on the peninsula that jutted out a little into the canal that ran along Eighty-Fourth Court behind Everglades Elementary. We fished, talked, and started fires. Fortunately, we didn't do the fires part very often.

I remember Gooney Golf and the driving range on Eighth Street, where the manager would give us a free Yoo-hoo beverage for picking up golf balls from around the perimeter of the driving range.

And who can forget Bird Bowl? I bowled in a league when I was younger and shot pool at night when I got older. Eric Clapton's "Cocaine" and "Lay Down Sally" played a lot in the pool room, but I think what I liked the most about Bird Bowl was the vanilla milkshakes at the snack bar.

I believe I only went to one movie at the Tropicaire Drive-In Theatre, but we spent many weekends there at the flea market, buying, selling, or just walking up and down those aisles that seemed to go on forever.

Then there were the restaurants like Arbetter's Hot Dogs. To this day, I still go there, and I even tried to turn my kids on to it. They pretend to like it, but I think they're just humoring me, they're really not into hot dogs. Believe it or not, I never went to Frankie's Pizza. I might be the only kid from Westchester who has never been there, but I sure heard a lot about it. I did go to the U-tote-M on Eighty-Seventh Avenue where we would go to grab an ICEE and some candy.

There are lots of great memories from Westchester, but none top the Shady Brew. The Shady Brew isn't a restaurant, a bar, or an amusement park, and you can't Google it. The only people who ever heard of it were the ones in our group, the neighborhood kids that hung out together every day.

My brothers and I, our neighbors, and our friends, would always meet at the Shady Brew. Every day, after school, we came home, changed clothes, and then went straight there. The Shady Brew was the spot where we'd meet to hang out, talk, and plan our next move. It was what we called the house on the corner, named for the large shade trees in the front yard and the homeowner who loved drinking beer. He didn't give us any of his beer; it wasn't that kind of place. You could always find a crowd at the Shady Brew, sitting on bikes, skateboards, the ground, or leaning against a car. Always.

We'd make fun of each other, talk about the previous day's shenanigans, the hard hits, the cheap shots, the bad passes, and the great catches. We were just a bunch of kids being kids. We'd imitate the Three Stooges, pretend we were wrestlers, have some tag team matches, the occasional boxing match, and sometimes we'd even have rock fights, using garbage can lids as shields. Maybe we weren't the smartest kids, but we did have fun. We played stickball and football in the street, and every couple of minutes someone would yell, "car," and we had to get out of the road to let traffic go by. We thought we were really smart as we sarcastically explained to the slow drivers where the gas pedal was.

Speaking of cars, if you had one, you thought twice about driving it down our street. There were lots of flying objects aimed at passing cars, tennis balls, golf balls, rocks, oranges, and grapefruits. Pretty much anything we could get our hands on. Once in a while, after a solid hit, the driver would stop, and the chase would be on. We were pretty quick, and we never got caught, but once, we left a skateboard behind, and it was taken as retribution. The poor ice cream man took so much abuse driving down our street, but he would come back every day.

The neighborhood stayed together for a long time, but around high school, people started moving. Most stayed nearby, some moved to Kendall, some to Palmetto, and a few left the state. I stayed friends with most of the old neighbors, but we seldom see each other, other than on social media. A few of us get together for birthdays, the occasional class reunion, and funerals.

As I watched my kids grow up, I couldn't help thinking about how much fun they would have had in Westchester.

Lee Goldwich

Lee Goldwich in his Westchester Optimist football uniform.

7 | A Great Place to Live

Westchester was a great place to live and grow up. It had a real hometown feel, and everyone knew their neighbors and helped each other out. We played all afternoon and into the evening and once school let out, we were outside with our friends until Mom called us in for our baths, dinner, and homework.

My grandparents initially purchased the house we lived in as their home, where their extended family could also live with them and support each other. The realtor was the mother of a classmate of ours. Her mom's business was on the corner of Coral Way and Eighty-Fourth Avenue, just down the street from our home, situated directly behind the Westchester Shopping Center back in 1965. Once I had a grasp of what things actually cost, it stuck in my mind that they paid $18,500 for a four bedroom, two bath home. Unbelievable!

The house was solid. It withstood numerous hurricanes and tropical storms and it was like Grand Central with all the kids from our block going in and out at all hours. The kids all loved hanging out at our place, and we played every game under the sun, jacks, hopscotch, dodge ball, red rover, Simon says, jump rope, climbed trees, sack races, Clackers, bicycle races, skateboarding, doing cartwheels and backbends, and playing on our swing set.

We lay on the grass and played "guess what that cloud looks like." We caught lady bugs, baked cookies and treats, and played so many more fun games and enjoyed activities.

The boys on the block even painted a football field on the street complete with the yard lines and end zones. Our house was on the fifty-yard line, and the girls would cheer for their favorite team. We'd put on plays, skits, and dance numbers on the step up from our living room area leading to the bedrooms. We'd send out invitations with entrance passes to the parents and set up chairs in our living room for our audience.

It was a time when we could leave our windows open and our doors unlocked without a care. We lived in that house that gave us such wonderful memories up until the last of us four sisters got married and moved out to our own places. My sisters and I often reminisce about the wonderful life we had as Westchester Kids!

Unfortunately, I can't bring myself to drive down our old block because I know it's not the same. I suppose I want to remember it as it was back when we were young in the '60s, '70s, and '80s.

I have so many things to say about our amazing school, Everglades Elementary, which left an indelible mark, along with memories I will forever cherish.

I was a transfer student from a local private school, St. Brendan Elementary, in second grade, so I didn't get the full effect of attending the school like my three sisters who followed me did. They were able to experience the whole shebang, from kindergarten through sixth grade, at our beloved school.

I was, nonetheless, accepted with open arms, in a caring and nurturing manner by teachers and the school's administration, making my transition as seamless as possible, and quashing my daunting fear of the unknown.

Attending a public school meant not having to wear the parochial school uniform every day, a light blue, belted dress hemmed to fall below my knees, with the stitched "St. B" monogram on the left breast pocket.

Ana Diaz Alvarez, 2, with big sister, Elizabeth Diaz Rizo, 4, in the front yard of their Westchester home.

My studies at Everglades commenced with Mrs. Brookman, third grade was with Mrs. Glass in the "six-pack," a building that housed six classes under air conditioning. Fourth grade was with Mrs. Joffee, fifth with Mr. Holberg, and I had sixth grade, my absolute favorite school year, with our amazing teacher, Mrs. Sparks, who, to date, is the biggest Miami Dolphins fan I've ever known. She was such a motivational and inspiring teacher, and she truly left a lasting impression on me.

I cherish all of the friends I made. We all got along and looked out for each other. I was on the safety patrol and took that responsibility very seriously, wearing my plastic neon orange colored sash and shiny silver badge with pride. The best was having the honor of hoisting the American flag up the flagpole at the start of the day and standing at attention while reciting the Pledge of Allegiance and singing the National Anthem.

While in Girl Scouts I sold their cookies door-to-door. My mom was a troupe co-leader when my sister Ana was a Brownie. She was also a room mother at school. We made plenty of pressed cookies and frosted cupcakes as classroom treats, which, sadly, in this day and age, is no longer permitted.

There was a great variety of wholesome food served in our cafeteria, which also doubled as our auditorium. The sign over the entrance doors read "Cafetorium" because it had a raised stage and backstage curtains, to host performances, presentations, and screen movies, in addition to the tables and chairs to eat our lunches at.

One day while on that cafeteria stage during the sixth grade talent show, I remember looking out into an audience of my peers, parents, teachers, and staff, as I sang the song "Killing Me Softly" wearing a floor-length white dress with yellow gingham trim. My friend Leonor accompanied me, strumming her guitar on a wooden stool, while my other friend (and Leonor's neighbor) Mimi struck her tambourine at just the right moments. All the while, butterflies were fluttering in my belly, but we pulled it off without a hitch. We even collaborated that summer before heading off to middle school and wrote our own songs and theatrical plays to entertain ourselves and pass the time.

Many other fond memories took place in that cafeteria. The Spaghetti Dinner PTA fundraisers were the best. I had fun serving the dinner trays to the families and then collecting them once they finished while wearing an apron over my Sunday best. Some dads even offered tips, which I graciously declined.

There was also the time some flying termites appeared in the dimly lit room where one would drop off the empty melamine lunch trays and use the back door of that room to exit the cafeteria. The kids were all screaming as they dodged the swarm of termites which seemed to cover the terrazzo floor like a rug. After that incident, the school immediately tented for the insects.

I recall when the '72 presidential election was held. Everglades Elementary was a local precinct, and all the voting booths were lined up outside in the school's entrance corridor. It was adjacent to the cafeteria, which had metal louvers and jalousie windows for ventilation — no central A/C in those days.

Voters were showing up in droves, waiting patiently in line to occupy one of the booths to cast their vote. During our lunch period, I remember that one kid started a chant: "Nixon! Nixon! Nixon!" Soon the entire cafeteria filled with kids erupting in the same chant. Even as youngsters, we were exercising our freedom of speech. Back then, I thought we'd made an impact in the outcome of the election, because of our chant. We were high-fiving each other the next day after the results came back in favor of Nixon.

We had our share of bullies, I can't deny. I had the unfortunate luck of having one of them home in on me in third grade. During our recess, he'd chase me until he caught me and would throw me down on the ground and sit on me, holding down my hands above my head, saying horrible things. I think all the kids were terrified of him. Therefore, if they saw what was happening, they most likely stayed away for fear of retaliation. Thankfully, a parent-teacher meeting ensued, and much to my relief, the bullying ceased.

I remember my favorite science project making papier-mâché planets of our solar system. I hung them up on a wire hanger in my room at the conclusion of the science fair. One not so thrilling project was bringing home a white mouse to care for. The mouse ended up eating its way through the cardboard box I'd transported him home in after placing it on top of the refrigerator overnight. Needless to say, my mom, grandmother, and sisters were not too pleased the next day when "Squeaky" was nowhere to be found.

While in sixth grade, I had the privilege of officiating at the "wedding" of two of my friends under the monkey bars on our playground during recess. I even created the invitations and decorations.

I also had the honor of having been selected by our music teacher, Mr. Dan Felcoski, along with some of my chorus classmates, to record all the songs that were used on the floats during the Junior Orange Bowl Parade held in Coral Gables before New Year's Eve. This was done at the Criterion Studios in North Miami where KC and the Sunshine Band and the Bee Gees recorded many of their tracks. It was quite awesome to record them with the former Miss America Vonda Van Dyke and the master of ceremonies for the annual pageant, Burt Parks. On the day of the parade, which was televised, we were lucky enough to be riding on the opening float with Miss Van Dyke and Mr. Parks.

Every now and then, on those rare occasions, when I smell someone wearing the perfume White Shoulders, I think of our fearless leader and principal, Mrs. Kazer. It was her signature fragrance, which lingered long after she left the room during her daily rounds, and I think warmly of her and her demeanor, her grace, and elegance I greatly admired. The memories and friends made while attending the best school a kid could have learned and grown up at, Everglades Elementary, are some of the fondest I have.

As far as restaurants, Westward Ho! was awesome. I used to buy their braided Challah bread with the cornmeal baked on the bottom. It was the best! When I got my car and driver's license in high school, I'd venture out a little farther west on Bird Road and frequent Godfather's Pizza with my friends. Their pizza was the bomb!

At Miami Coral Park Senior High, I didn't attend my senior prom, because I had a long distance relationship with my boyfriend at the time. He lived in New York, and it would have been unheard of if I'd gone to the prom while he was up north. We eventually broke up that summer, but I ended up going to my new boyfriend's prom the following year. In the middle of all of the festivities, Ms. Eads came up to the mic and had the music stopped while everyone was on the dance floor to announce that the prom was ending immediately. The McDuffie riots had started that evening and they wanted everyone to get home safely from the Sonesta Hotel in Key Biscayne. Chaos ensued and parents were calling the hotel because there were no cell phones back then. I guess me going to proms was never meant to be!

Elizabeth Diaz Rizo

8 | El Gringo de las Calles de "Wecheter"

I truly believe I had a unique, cultural experience growing up in "Wecheter" (how it is fondly called by the Cubans in Westchester). The word cultural sounds so cerebral though; it was much more physical and verbal, and full of strong relationships. I'm a Jewish-American man whose main circle of friends were the Cuban guys and girls in my neighborhood; *mis amigos de las calles* (my friends from the streets). It was primarily about being friends, and secondarily that we had different cultures.

My first memories are of my brother and me playing football in the streets with the boys and sitting in the front yard talking with the girls, who I came to realize were Cuban, that's how it began. As I was invited into homes where the moms didn't speak English but was welcomed with Cuban crackers (galletas) *con* Coca Cola, or later, with *café con leche* (strong coffee with milk), I naturally assimilated into a different way of thinking, talking, and acting.

One had to be tough growing up on the streets with the boys. You also had to be good in sports and you had to expect to be called names if you messed up, and other names they just called you in general. We had to stand our ground, but it helped us develop into men. I've seen many of these guys over the years, and I'm happy to say we older men look great and have stayed in excellent shape, influenced by our experiences in the streets and sports fields.

I must also mention the girls as well, because I never got over my first crushes on the ones living across the street. Anyone I liked after that had to have some of the traits my first loves had, which is a theme that remained throughout the romantic parts of my life. But let me say, I thought much more about friendships than differences, because they were my friends.

So, fast forward through the years of Rockway Junior High School and Miami Coral Park Senior High School where my classmates knew me as a Jewish-American guy. It was after high school that my American life became *mi vida Cubano* as *el Gringo*. Soon after high school, I met and married a Cuban girl ... not just a random Cuban girl, but one from our high school, whose brother I knew from Coach Parker's PE Class.

Her parents were deeply entrenched in guarijo Cuban culture (a Cuban from the country-side or farmer), and at first, I was viewed with skepticism, but since I had a good friendship with my future brother-in-law, I was accepted into the family. It was during this time I was fondly known as el Gringo.

In the years before I understood and spoke Spanish, I would hear ... *el Gringo dice this ... el Gringo hace that* ... so it was really important for me to learn Spanish, but it was so much more than learning the language. The food, the parties, and the life events that were now my life were Cuban. I learned how to prepare and cook lechon entero (a whole pig). I learned things about Cuban music including salsa, merengue, Punto Guajiro, la clave, El Buena Vista Social Club, and Celia Cruz. I even helped my father-in-law on his yuca farm by harvesting, boxing, and driving his produce to the Sedano's Supermarkets. He was the most hard-core Cuban guy I ever met, and that's saying something, because I had come from a neighborhood of hard-core Cuban guys.

Both my daughters were influenced by an abuela who was deeply rooted in Cuban culture and spoke only Spanish, so they ate homemade Cuban food regularly and naturally learned Spanish. There are many cousins, aunts, and uncles, who throughout the years, have visited or emigrated from Cuba, and my oldest daughter has visited the family farm back in Cuba. My daughter continues passing her Cuban culture onto my grandkids because she and their abuela (Abu), speak Spanish to them and make *comida típica* Cubano (typical Cuban food) for them. And the grandkid who can already talk knows how to speak Spanish.

As for myself, I use my Westchester experience to help me in my teaching career. Of course, my Spanish is much better, so I can help all the Latino students and their parents with the details of education here and can teach any topic I know in Spanish. Over the years, I've learned much about *caña de azucar* (sugar cane) and farming in general. I have hands-on knowledge of the canal system we had running through our neighborhood and use this information as an Agricultural and Environmental Educator.

My experiences in Westchester have made me an environmental educator in the workings of the Everglades National Park and the drainage basin to which it's connected. Because Westchester is so close to the Everglades, my father regularly took us out to extremely remote places along Tamiami Trail and the canal. We walked on old forgotten roads which had overgrown with vegetation, climbed the water locks, tubes, and levees, and fished all along the canals toward Naples.

I continue to visit places so few people know of, except those of us who lived near there. When we were kids, the canal system was everywhere. There were

Mike Moss at the Big Cypress National Preserve just west of Everglades National Park.

borrow pits filled with water, teaming with aquatic life at the base of every expressway exit. Sometimes, we'd see manatees and otters under the bridges crossing the canals. We'd find turtles and snakes, many of which are now classified as an endangered species. This same canal system stretches all the way across Tamiami Trail, through the Everglades, and affects the flow and quality of the water we use every day. So, it's important that our elected officials have a good plan and promise to care for our water management system.

That is how growing up in Westchester has affected me and still does to this day and will continue to influence me. I am proud to be *el Gringo de las Calles de* "Wecheter."

Mike Moss

9 | The Things We Got Away With

My senior year at Miami Coral Park Senior High School, the '78 to '79 school year, was epic and memorable in many ways. We had so many good times. I used to hang out with my best friend, and we had many of the same classes. I still can't believe how much crap we pulled.

In honors government class, the bulk of our grade was based on a semester-long project, in which we had to compare and contrast two congressmen. We were to work in pairs, and my friend and I, working together, chose to compare Bob Dole, a conservative from Kansas, to Henry "Scoop" Jackson, a liberal from Washington. We spent about twelve hours working on it together, hand-writing a ten-page paper, of course, overnight, the night before it was due!

Class started at 10:00 a.m., and we rushed to get to school with our completed assignments at 10:10 a.m. When the paper was returned to us, we had three points taken off for various problems, plus ten points taken off for being late, so we got an eighty-seven percent.

The next semester, we got the same task, comparing and contrasting two different congressmen. Knowing that our teacher had returned the assignment to us, and she had no way of retaining a copy of all those papers, we decided to plagiarize our own work. We chose the junior senators from the same states. They both had the same voting record as the senior senators, so we simply rewrote the bio for each, and transcribed the rest of the paper verbatim, correcting the three "mistakes" we previously made. Consequently, we received a one-hundred percent on the second term.

My friend and I used to skip the last period of school and go to Miami Jai-Alai for the matinee game once or twice a week. When the jai alai season ended, we didn't know what to do with ourselves, being somewhat addicted. So, we started playing amateur jai alai at Orbea's in Hialeah.

We also used to sneak into El Club de las Americas to play jai alai on their squash courts once they closed. On one occasion there, an elderly man, walking with a cane, came and yelled at us in Spanish for being there. We just ignored him until he pulled a dagger out of the top of his cane and started brandishing it in our direction. That got us out of there quickly.

I used to skip class so often that my accounting class teacher warned me that, in the future, should I miss class, I must have an excuse note from my parents. I went home that day, knowing that my dad would play along. I wrote five different notes with five different excuses. My father signed them all, and the next time I skipped my accounting class, I brought all five notes in the following day. When my teacher asked me if I had a note from my parents, I fanned them out and said, "Take your pick."

As you can guess, I was sent to the principal's office, but no action was taken since my father had legitimately signed them. The pen was mightier than the principal's binoculars used to spot students skipping class! Back then, parents had the last say. Things are a little different these days.

My friend and I also had honors history class together out in one of the portable classrooms. Again, in pairs, our major assignment was to present a historical reenactment in front of the class, and I don't think there were any other parameters. I came up with the brilliant idea of reenacting the *2000 Year Old Man*, a comedy skit originally improvised by Mel Brooks and Carl Reiner. We memorized the whole routine, and I still know it by heart. Needless to say, we got a D on that assignment.

Then there was math class. My partner in crime and I had taken Algebra/Trig in eleventh grade but dropped off the honors track to take Trig/Analytic Geometry in our senior year. The Trig semester was an exact repeat of the last semester of eleventh grade, so that was a breeze.

Never having gotten a grade lower than a B, we now found ourselves in analytic geometry in the last semester of our senior year. We were already accepted to the University of Florida and were suffering from acute senioritis. Our teacher would call out our scores to the entire class but had a very lenient policy of allowing students to retake a test if they were dissatisfied with their grade. My teacher would frequently say, "Dronsky, you failed the test. You want to take it again or let it ride?"

Same goes for my friend and our response was always the same, "Let it ride!"

I'm not going to go into detail about our chemistry class, but we had so many explosions we were all surprised no one died during that class. Had those types of experiments taken place today, it would have definitely met with some severe punishment.

Rick Dronsky (center), with his parents and sisters.

I also remember a few fun facts from my marine biology class. I worked at China Maid and brought into class a can of smoked marine eel I "borrowed" from the restaurant. This was before sushi was popular in this country, and no one could believe that eel was served commercially. Also, because of our interest in marine biology, I used to go snorkeling frequently with Spencer Green and Bill Medina.

On one adventure, they captured a tiny creature which we couldn't identify so we brought it to class and researched it, to no avail. Since they caught it, they named it a "Spedina." That name remains today, although it can't be found in any official guide-books or documentation.

Finally, I want to thank Jacqueline Gutstein for prompting us to dig up old memories, write these stories, and for compiling this book. She always was a class act back in Westchester, and, apparently, she still is today!

Rick Dronsky

10 | Friends, Girls, Music, and Sports

My family moved from California to Westchester in 1970. My childhood in Westchester was great and I had plenty of friends ... twelve boys in the neighborhood growing up together doing all sorts of incredible things. We rode our bikes everywhere and hung out from 8:00 a.m. to 8:00 p.m. during the summer months off from school. When we got home during the school period, Mom always had something for us to eat as most Latin mothers do. It was her way of maintaining a happy family.

Homework was a must at the house, but I took advantage of having a Spanish-speaking mom that didn't understand completely how things were in school. After homework, I went out to play all types of sports and our group always came up with new games to play. We were always looking for wild things to do as young boys do. Throughout my youth I played various sports at Tamiami Park, Flagami Park, was in Los Cubanitos Baseball League, and hung out with the boys.

At school we spoke like tough guys did back then and did numerous things that most likely would not be accepted today. I was also lazy regarding bookwork, but notorious for playing the "I don't understand the question or the work," and had my smarter friends to do the work for me.

During the summer months and beginning at the age of eleven, I gained some work experience with my dad at his carpentry shop and then later at the body shop. It was just a thing I had to do with no questions asked, and for very long hours since my dad was a workaholic.

Once I was able to get away from under dad's work routine, I faked my age and worked at a fast food joint. I was fourteen years old and had a manager who was super cool. We'd get blasted together on the weekends after work, and as young people do, we really thought we were cool back then.

I began to drive my dad's Ford station wagon when I was fifteen years old in and around the driveway and had to wash it on Sundays for "visita time," when it was time to make visits to family and friends. Once I "borrowed" the car for a spin while dad went to feed the dogs at his shop. I thought I was so cool driving the car to my friend's house.

Trying to back out of their driveway, I accidentally ran over him while he was riding his bike. I was horrified, but, thankfully, my friend survived without a scratch. Unfortunately, his bike was destroyed. His brother was so angry with me that he broke the antenna on my dad's car. This wasn't good, because my dad took care of his things and wouldn't be happy. My friends came over later with their father, and I got in deep trouble, having to pay to fix his bike. Needless to say, I was punished and grounded for a good long while.

While in Banyan Elementary School, my bad behavior got me in trouble, and I was paddled a bunch of times by the PE coach. The school had a lot of strict rules and I managed to break them all, which also led to lots of detentions.

When I attended Rockway Junior High School, I had such a great time and got into all the sports that were available in order to get out of class. Being an adolescent, I had a lot of girlfriends, especially cheerleaders, but I was also involved in wrestling, basketball, softball, and took all the elective courses available. I even took cooking classes to eat all the great food. Although I really didn't learn much, I got to hang out with pretty girls.

Dances at the school were lots of fun and the local musical groups were great (Antiques, Coke, Heaven, Miami Sound Machine, and others). I had my own DJ business called Oui Disco from age fifteen to around eighteen. Other DJs and I would rent banquet halls and have Open House Dances, charging $5 per person. All the DJs would compete against each other during the night to see who could play the best music and get the most people to dance. I can also remember crashing numerous house parties and having a blast.

I have vivid memories of the stores in Westchester that we all went to mostly by bike when I was growing up including JByrons, Zayre, Kmart, Playworld, Luria's, Westchester Mall, and Midway Mall which was nearby. I also remember going to the Tropical Flea Market and Tropicaire Drive-In Theatre on Bird Road, and the Westchester Theatre. On Sundays, we'd also hang out at the theater near Coral Way and Ninety-Seventh Avenue. There were plenty of great restaurants I ate at including

Lum's, Pancake House, Frankie's Pizza, Mister Donut, Burger King, Arbetter's Hot Dogs, Castle Burger, Rio Cristal, Ferrari's Pizza, Nunzios, and the Pit Bar-B-Q.

I started a good friendship with a guy named Victor who was like a brother to me and who passed away in 2011. To this day, I miss him very much and think of all the great times we had together. He was a great person to have by your side. RIP my friend.

After high school, I met a beautiful lady and got married. I was young and immature, and although we had a wonderful son, we didn't stay together, but are very close friends to this day.

Rafael A. Cubela in the early '80s with his young son.

I've kept in touch with many of my friends, but it's often difficult to see each other because of our work schedules. I've passed by the old neighborhood numerous times, but my original house was knocked down and replaced.

What has always stayed with me are my memories of a loving household with two beautiful parents, whom I adored and were attentive to my sister and me. Growing up I learned how to treat others with respect by watching my parents and how they treated people, and for that I will be forever grateful.

Rafael A. Cubela

11 | Remembering Eddie

I'll never forget that morning. It was unusually cool for an early November morning, but not too unusual for a typical Miami fall day. Any change from the heat was fine by me.

I hated living in the heat of South Florida, and I often wished I could live up north in the cold and snow. Both of my parents had grown up in northern cities, so they knew the miseries of Chicago and Philadelphia winters, and that's why we lived here, but as I had never experienced it, I wanted it even more.

I'd gotten up early for school that day, partly because I couldn't sleep, but also because I was anxious to meet up with my friends so we could all ride over and take a look at the accident scene. We couldn't go see it the night before because our parents wouldn't let us. They said it wasn't courteous and that we should respect the family's wishes for seclusion and prayer.

My closest friends and I had gotten out of elementary school that past June and had just started junior high, what today would be called middle school. I was almost thirteen years old, and to this day, I cannot honestly explain what was going on inside my head when my friends and I silently glided our bikes to a stop at the spot where the accident had happened. The street was littered with used large blue flashbulbs, the old-fashioned kind that were ejected violently from a camera after being used.

My friends and I had spent the summer causing our usual mischief around the neighborhood—having pizzas delivered to people's houses when they didn't order them, making prank phone calls, hiding among the branches of tall ficus trees, and dropping leaves on passing cars. Just generally trying to be bad-asses while riding everywhere on our bikes. In those days, we were allowed to roam free on our bikes and our parents encouraged it. They told us to come home as soon as the streetlights came on. They had no worries about us or the world we lived in.

We'd ride to Miami International Airport to experience a low-flying jet going right over our heads before landing. We rode to the local strip mall that we called "the Store," to browse through Western Auto for bicycle tire repair kits. We rode to the Dipper Dan Ice Cream Shoppe to see if any new cute girls were working there. We shopped for cheap candy at Woolworths and we rode around to the back of the movie theater to try to hear the rated M movie from behind the locked exit doors. A childhood without cell phones, video games, and only four channels on TV left us with a lot of time to use our imaginations outdoors.

We also spent a lot of time lighting fires in our backyards using plastic toy models, dried up leaves, or anything else we thought would burn. While I was an amateur firebug, limiting myself to immolating in minutes my WWII models I'd spent untold weeks building, painting and perfecting, my closest buddies specialized in small primitive bombs. These ranged from blowing up straws packed full of gunpowder taken from cap gun ammo to igniting saltpeter, a principal ingredient in gunpowder, mixed with sugar in a plastic gallon milk jug.

The latter would send a stream of gray smoke ninety feet into the air. The neighbors had to call the fire department on me one time when I accidentally set my tree house on fire. Once, my friends escaped before the cops could catch them after they started a conflagration in a trash dumpster full of popcorn grease behind the theater.

One of my other buddies was Steve. He lived down the block with his mom and dad, his big sister Nancy, and his little brother Eddie. Steve was one of my best friends. His birthday was the day after mine, so every year as our respective birthdays approached, we planned on going to each other's parties.

We talked about how cool it was that we were friends and that we were not only both named Steve, but that we had birthdays one day apart. I always kidded him about being older because mine was the nineteenth, and his was the twentieth. We were really close. His sister was three years older than us and in my sister's grade, and his little brother Eddie, at eight years old, was the youngest of us all.

Eddie was always trying to be one of us. Always wanting to do what we were doing, always wanting to go where we were going. He was a pain sometimes, and we teased him a lot, but we knew he really was a good kid.

Although I only saw Steve one more time after that awful morning, to this day, I always think of him on his birthday. One year, some fifteen years after the accident, I'd returned from performing on the road with my band, and my dad gave me a message that Steve had called me on my birthday but left no number. He must have been thinking about me too.

There we all were, on that cool morning back then, just a few days after Halloween, trying to comprehend the incomprehensible. We were trying to understand what we were feeling, and what Steve's little brother Eddie might have felt.

This was where it had happened. This was where Eddie died. I could see the blood still slightly glistening as the asphalt absorbed it. There was a large patch at the center on the street, with a thin trailing stream, now dried, running down into the grass by the side of the road.

He'd been hit at dusk on the previous evening by a man driving a small work van. I was told Eddie had been on his way back from the store when he emerged from between two cars parked on the swale. The driver never saw him, let alone had time to hit the brakes. He knocked Eddie off his bike while going at least thirty-five miles an hour, killing him instantly. Eddie was only eight years old.

We found out later that the van's driver was the owner of a hardware store located just a few miles from where we all lived. He was driving home from work like any other ordinary day, not knowing his life was about to be altered as irrevocably as ours.

Those damn flashbulbs bothered me. I couldn't understand why anyone would be taking pictures of such a horrible thing. I found out much later that since it had been considered a crime scene, it was standard procedure for the police to have a photographic record for evidence. It needed to be documented.

Secretly, I wanted to see what that camera saw, although I couldn't imagine why. I thought later that maybe it was because I never got to see Eddie again, that would have been a way of saying goodbye.

To this day, I can still envision those burned out bulbs lying there on the road, crushed by passing cars whose drivers slowed down to look.

Before my parents passed, I'd driven by the spot where Eddie had died a thousand times since that day, on my way to visit them at their house, the one they'd bought in 1956 and lived in until their passing. There was never a Drive Safely plaque at the spot, nor was there ever a hastily erected memorial sign.

There were never any stuffed teddy bears, wilted flowers, balloons, or votive candles as there would be today. It's almost as though the whole thing never happened. I'll always remember though; it will never escape me. Whether I see that spot at night, in the daytime, or at any time of the year, I'll never forget.

There are times when I think about one other day too. The last time I saw Steve. That early November afternoon was unusually warm in the small cemetery in the center of town.

I ignored the sweat running down my back inside my new black suit, felt the heat on my shoes, and watched that white casket being lowered into the ground. I wasn't aware until that moment that there were caskets made that small.

Photo credit: Steve Moss

This is the street where eight-year-old, Eddie,
was struck and killed by a van
in November 1971.

With the exception of the nearly inaudible voice of
the rabbi as he read the prayers, I remember how quiet it
was with only the sound of the wind rustling the leaves on
the ground, and the mockingbirds and sparrows
chattering innocently in the trees around me.

I often wander back to those times in my mind, but
especially back to that day, probably more than I should. I
guess I go there not only to try and relive what I didn't
realize I was living then, but also to try and put my

present life into perspective. I go there to try to remember what is really important, and what is not. And maybe, just maybe, I go there to live a little bit for Eddie too, who never really got the chance to live at all.

Steve Moss

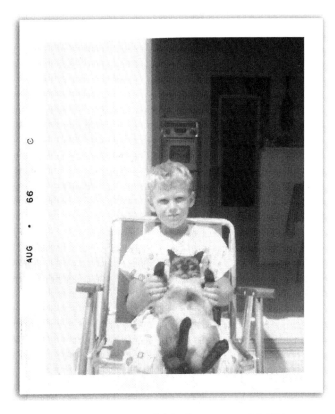

*Steve Moss, age 7, with his Siamese cat, Mei-Ling,
outside his Westchester home in 1966.*

12 | From Cuba to Westchester

My parents were both born in Cuba, although my father's family came from Radziłów, Poland, and my mother's family was primarily from Spain and Portugal. When they fled Communist Cuba in 1961, they went to Costa Rica for several months with me in the belly and then flew to South Florida. I always say I was made in Cuba and born in the USA.

When they arrived in Miami, my parents stayed at the Cactus Motel for a week with the money they saved working in Costa Rica, but it was too expensive and within a week, they found a more affordable apartment to rent. I was born at Mount Sinai Hospital in Miami Beach a month after my parents arrived in Miami. They wanted me to have an American name, so they named me Jacqueline after the first lady at the time, Jacqueline Kennedy. Our family later moved to a duplex near Little Havana and when a close friend told my parents there was a house for sale down the street from them in a newly formed neighborhood called Westchester, my parents took the plunge and bought the house.

The decision to move to Westchester changed our lives and shaped who I became. We moved into a three

*An advertisement in The Miami News, 1958, for new homes
in Coral Park Estates, the neighborhood around Sixteenth
Street and Eighty-Seventh Avenue in the new
neighborhood called Westchester.*

*The Gutstein family moved into the Bel Mar model,
a three bedroom, two bath home in 1967 and
lived there until 1981.*

bedroom, two bath home with a great backyard that was lined with orange, lime, and mango trees. The front door had white wooden diamond shaped décor that was very popular in the '60s and it had a screen door that we used all the time.

I remember hand-squeezing a laundry basket full of fresh orange juice which tasted amazing. Our mangos were out of this world, and that tree became my refuge when I wanted to be alone with my thoughts. Some afternoons when I climbed onto my mango tree perch, I pretended it was a ship out in the middle of the ocean and climbed to different branches to get a better glimpse of the sea.

In our backyard, we also played tackle football with our friends and practiced hitting a ball with our wooden bat. It would also be where we laid out our Slip 'N Slide and erected many portable pools that increasingly got larger as we grew older.

At the far back corner of the backyard, we had an L shaped concrete area where our metal trash cans were stored. Mind you, these cans didn't have wheels, and when it was garbage day, we had to drag those bins from the back corner of the yard all the way to the front yard. Who in the world thought that was a good idea?

Our house had the typical Floridian white pebble roof, wall air conditioner units, and terrazzo floors that were mopped using *el palo con trapo* (the Cuban style wooden stick with a mop cloth). This style of floor was easy to clean and maintain and made for great sliding competitions when we wore our socks.

We also had a screened-in Florida room where my brothers and I and our friends spent most of the day playing darts, ping-pong, drawing on our blackboard, and hanging out to chill.

Jacqueline Gutstein, Abuela Rosa and Margarita Gutstein enjoying their screened-in Florida room.

Our *World Encyclopedia* collection that my parents bought from a salesman who walked up to the house was at the end of the bedroom hallway, and a yellow rotary phone was attached to the wallpapered kitchen wall.

There was a utility room where we had our washer and dryer and where my parakeets, fish, gerbil, chicks, mice, and turtles would live at different times throughout the year. This was the room where we kept our outdoor toys, football, bat, baseballs, baseball gloves, and kickball.

We played mostly outside, and we came home sweaty and hungry when the streetlights came on.

My younger brother was only two when we moved to Westchester, so we had a cloth diaper delivery service that came to our house once a week, and a real-life milkman who left cold milk bottles in our metal grate container right outside our front door on the porch.

The front of my home had a long row of bushes right outside the bedroom windows with a little walkway behind it, so it was a great place for hiding out. We bought slingshots from the ice cream truck and got these hard berries from our trees and had yard to yard sling shot competitions. When one of those berries hit you, you definitely felt it and the welt would be enormous.

One of the best presents my brothers and I received one year for the holidays was a microscope. I spent endless hours collecting bugs, grass, and anything I could fit on the slides to view in all its magnified glory. I also treasured a magnifying glass I had that slid open and closed in a vinyl sleeve. You could catch me sitting on my lawn on a hot sunny day trying to make a blade of grass burn with the reflection from the sun using my magnifying glass or burning holes in old newspapers with the power of the sun. Maybe I watched one too many survival programs as a child.

On our block, our friends and my family were the only two Cuban families living there when we moved in. Actually, both our families were Jewish Cubans (fondly known as Jewbans) and as the years went by, more and more Cubans and Jewish Cubans moved into the neighborhood. It was convenient to walk to Temple Or Olom which was only two blocks away and where my brothers had their Bar Mitzvahs, and I was confirmed in the Jewish religion.

The sidewalk in front of our house also provided endless opportunities for entertainment. We'd play hopscotch and roller skate in our adjustable metal skates. One day the bolts on the skates got loose and it opened up and I took a nasty fall.

I had a cap gun that I loved to shoot with and pretend I was a policewoman. I also took the red paper strips filled with gun powder and used a hammer to smash them on the sidewalk, making cool popping sounds.

It was on the sidewalk where my brothers and I learned how to ride a bicycle. One day as I was riding my bike down the block with my training wheels on, one accidentally fell off, and I was forced to either balance the bike or crash. I was pleasantly surprised when I kept on riding with no problem. I was elated, and road back home to officially remove the other training wheel and off I went. I had a blue girls bike with a white banana seat, high rise cruiser bars with plastic strips hanging down from the ends of the handle-bar stuck into the little hole at the end of the rubber hand grips.

There was a metal basket affixed to the handlebars, a horn, a bell, and a small license plate on the back of my seat with my name on it. My bike had all the comforts and accessories a kid could want. We also had a little bright red plastic car that I rode around in with a steering wheel and a trunk that opened up. It moved on foot power, but to me, it felt like I was driving a Rolls Royce!

Our house had a carport, where these large planks of wood were stacked on the underside of the carport ceiling, leaving about six inches of open space. Birds would build their nests on these planks throughout the year, and I'd use a ladder to go up and take a peek at the eggs, and eventually, the new hatchlings. We also had cardinals that made nests in our rose bushes right outside our Florida room every year that we watched in awe.

My mom drove a white Mercury Comet with blue interior for a while, and my dad had a Buick Skylark that I used to learn to drive when I was fifteen years old and got a learners permit.

I remember when we purchased a wood paneled station wagon my Cuban parents would call *el pisicorre*, meaning you step on the pedal, and it would go fast. My brothers and I loved to sit in the back seats that faced each other, without seat belts of course, which were not the norm back then.

Max Gutstein, 2, and Jacqueline Gutstein, 6, in the driveway of their Westchester home in 1967.

Later, my parents purchased a four-door Ford Maverick and then a silver Buick Riviera that was really sharp looking.

When I turned five, I attended Everglades Elementary School. Years later I was part of the safety patrol unit and got to wear an orange belt and sash with a silver badge pinned to it. When it was raining, we wore bright yellow raincoats and black rubber boots which made us look really professional. As a small child, I dreamed of becoming a policewoman one day, so being on the safety patrol was a big deal for me, and I swore to myself no child or parent was going to get hit by a car on my watch!

My fondest memory in elementary school is of my third grade teacher, Mrs. Hardy, whom I had the pleasure of recently speaking with after fifty-three years. Mrs. Hardy's class was in the newly constructed air-conditioned building housing six classrooms called the *six-pack*. I volunteered to be her class helper, and she was the most sweetest and caring teacher I knew.

I also joined the chorus although I couldn't sing worth a damn. To save face, the music teacher had me play the tambourine and told me to sing when the entire chorus sung, probably to drown out my off-key vocals. I enjoyed physical education the most, running relays, climbing the monkey bars, and playing kickball.

In fifth grade, I was put into a class with both fifth and sixth graders, and it was then I played footsies for the first and only time, in the library with an older kid and learned about the birds and the bees from my classmates. Yes, those years were indeed amazing.

After that, I attended Rockway Junior High School, while most of my friends went to West Miami Junior High because of where the school boundaries were. I met some new friends at Rockway, but those three years might as well have been ten since my old friends from Everglades Elementary and I grew apart.

I attended Miami Coral Park Senior High School as a sophomore from 1977-1979. I remember Elvis Presley passed away the first year I was there.

On January 19, 1977, it snowed in Miami and I remember opening the front door of the house that morning and being in awe at the white covered lawn and cars. All the neighbors were outside in their pajamas and robes staring at this incredible event. What a sight that was!

At Miami Coral Park, I reunited with a lot of my old Everglades friends, which was great. I enjoyed being on the bowling team and participating in badminton competitions at numerous schools. My favorite times, however, were my art and photography classes with my awesome teachers, Tom Wyroba, Ivy Edmunds, and my printing and photography teacher, Coach Adams.

Mr. Wyroba brought a unique perspective to art class as did Miss Edmunds, my other art teacher. She even brought a real motorcycle for a drawing project and propped it atop several desks in the middle of the classroom for her students to draw. They were amazing teachers and these classes taught me photography and graphic arts, which I used in my early work experiences.

On the last day of school in 1979, a group of students released seventy-nine mice throughout the school, and all day long, you would hear sporadic screams every time someone saw one of the mice scurrying the hallways. This infamous stunt made the news, and I don't believe the culprits, who were eventually identified, were allowed to attend the graduation ceremony.

Since I lived one block in front of Miami Coral Park Senior High School on Seventeenth Street, the back of the school and the field was where I hung out with my two best friends. I played tennis there with my wooden Davis racket I purchased with my S&H Green Stamps and played paddle ball and racquetball on their courts. I even tried some hoops on the basketball court, ran the track, and walked the field with some older friends I met there. It was my extended childhood playground.

On weekends and during the summer months, my family practically lived at the YM-YWHA on Eighth Street. It had a country club style setting with a huge swimming pool, cabanas, and food areas. My mother recalls us being there on weekends from when it opened to when it closed, and this is where I learned to swim and compete on their

Jacqueline Gutstein with her brother Max at the YM-YWHA pool.

swim team. All the Jewish families in the neighborhood went there ... it was the place to be and meet friends. It was there I made so many beautiful memories with my family and friends.

We used to shop at Food Fair, Eckerd Drugs, and the little magazine store sandwiched in between. Carousel Salon was the beauty parlor my mom would go to, and I would frequent Lum's for their Lumburger and the Westchester Theatre was where we would see all the latest movies. We shopped at JByrons, Kmart, and the air-conditioned Westchester Mall that was attached to those stores and where I bought my first Ken Rosewall tennis shoes with his signature on the sides.

On the west side of Coral Way and Eighty-Seventh Avenue was Zayre, where I got my first job as a cashier that lasted two weeks, IHOP, and the Amoco Gas Station our friend owned and my family frequented. Back then the attendant would pump your gas, clean your windshield, and check your tires, and you didn't even have to get out of the car. Now, that was service!

My family members were avid bowlers, so most of our birthday parties were held at Bird Bowl on Ninety-Second Avenue and Bird Road. We also went to pick up staples like bread, milk, and Napolitano ice cream at *La Vaquita* as we Cubans referred to it, formerly known as Farm Stores. Every time we returned from a vacation, we knew we were getting close to home, because we would drive by *La Vaquita,* and we kids would scream its name with joy.

Another big thrill was when the air-conditioned Traveling Library bookmobile would park near Firestone off Eighty-Seventh Avenue. I was there for hours at a time looking at all the books, and mind you, it was only the size of a recreational RV. I always had books to return, and more books to check out. My brothers and I would bike to these shopping centers without a care in the world and return home to eat dinner and then go back out around the neighborhood, sometimes late into the evening. It was safe to do so back then, and we normally had the front door open with just the screen door to hold back the mosquitoes.

Westchester was this small slice of heaven that was filled with families and kids, and lots of love. I thank my parents for raising me there and for all the Westchester Kids who were a huge part of my life. I wouldn't trade my upbringing for anything in the world.

Jacqueline Gutstein

13 | A Wholesome Youth

My family arrived in Miami from Cuba in 1968 when I was six and I lived in Westchester most of my childhood into my teens.

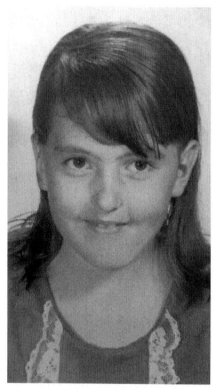

Maria E. Garcia-Casals

My parents, two brothers, and I lived with my godfather who owned a large house behind Everglades Elementary School along with my grandmother, aunt, uncle, and two cousins.

Years later, we moved into our own house on the same block. Our other aunt and her husband and their four daughters also lived near us along with my three other cousins and their parents who lived near Miami Coral Park Senior

High School. It was nice to have so much family nearby and we would gather at one house or another for birthdays and weekend visits.

We were a total of twelve cousins, all around the same age, so our parents would take us shopping to Publix, JByrons, and Luria's. We'd collect S&H Green Stamps from the supermarkets and redeem the booklets at the S&H Store. The store was like a large warehouse full of household items, and they also had a pamphlet for you to select your items depending on how many stamps you had to redeem.

My favorite store was Luria's because that's where I purchased my first watch, and they had a layaway plan for us to make affordable payments. The watch was a Movado, which was popular at the time. The best restaurant was Lila's, where they had the famous steak and fries, and I can't forget the Batido de Mamey (mamey milkshake).

I remember one weekend going to watch a scary movie at the midnight show at the Westchester Theatre with my best friend, her younger brother, and his friend. The movie was terrifying and featured a large white car that would follow people. On the ride home, as we approached my friend's house to drop off her and her brother, we noticed a white car, similar to the one in the movie, with the engine on but with the lights off just sitting on the swale. We started screaming and, needless to say, we kept going and circled the neighborhood for over an hour until the white car finally left and my friends and I were dropped off. Our friend who was driving that night eventually ran out of gas circling the neighborhood and was unable to make it home. His parents had to come and get him after he phoned them from a nearby pay phone. It was such a strange and scary coincidence, and I never forgot it.

After junior high, I attended Miami Coral Park Senior High School and made a lot of new friends. My favorite class was graphics and printing class with Coach Adams. We had a real darkroom where we'd develop our own film. One of our projects was to create a working pinhole camera from a shoebox, which was really neat. We also made silk screen artwork and printed the images on our T-shirts.

As far as sports went, I enjoyed being on the badminton team and I played junior varsity volleyball. I remember taking Drivers Education class in the parking lot where they placed orange cones all around and we learned how to parallel park. My first car was a Galaxy 500 that I totaled in a car wreck. It was pretty disheartening, but I was lucky to walk away from the accident.

After school, my best friend, my cousin, and I would play racquetball and hang out in the back of the school. I got my first job for school credit at Kmart as a stockperson and cashier. My friends and I would skip some classes once in a while to have breakfast at IHOP and go to the beach. It was just the thing to do. My cousins and I belonged to a religious youth group at St. Brendan's Catholic Church where we'd gather on weekends, hold fundraising events, and also had dances and carwashes to raise money for the church. I also remember El Club de las Americas where I did some modeling and took etiquette classes.

Looking back on my youth, living and growing up in Westchester was an innocent and fun time. We could leave our doors unlocked and had no fears or worries. Living in Westchester, surrounded by my extended family and great friends, shaped who I became as an adult. I will be forever grateful for my parents who sacrificed a lot to give my brothers and I a wonderful upbringing.

Maria E. Garcia-Casals

14 | A Special Place in My Heart

Westchester, the great neighborhood with endless memories, will always have a special place in my heart. That little town, which I was born and raised in, provided me with friends for life. Although I got married in Maryland, six of the eight groomsmen in my wedding were friends from Westchester, and to this day, we continue to be best friends. I haven't been back there in several years because our family home of more than fifty years was recently sold and most of the special places I loved no longer exist, but when I did go, it brought back special memories as I picture the landmarks that once occupied these spots.

Looking back, you'd think I spent all my early childhood years at the Westchester Shopping Center, which left quite an impression on me as a kid. Both of my parents worked, so whenever there was a day off from school, my grandparents would pick up my brother and me and take us to Burger Castle, Westward Ho!, or Lum's (who could forget the Ollie Burger) for lunch. To this day, I still think back to when I walked into Westward Ho! and saw the fire and steam rising from the stoves and the chefs wearing those tall white chef hats.

We had frequent family gatherings, which always included a bunch of cousins, and after our meals, my grandparents would take all the kids to Dipper Dan for an ice cream. What a treat!

My favorite place that my dad took us to was Royal Castle, which was across the street from West Miami Junior High School. I loved sitting at the counter and spinning around on those orange bar stools that were mounted on the floor. It was also neat watching the cooks flip the burgers, then throw the chopped onions on top, before placing them on the buns. Their hamburgers were delicious!

Mike Moss (left) with Evan Moss (right).

My best memories as a kid were of getting woken up before the sun came up and fishing with my dad and my brother, Mike, almost every Saturday. Nothing could replace those experiences. Most of the time, we'd trail our boat east to Dinner Key Marina in Coconut Grove. Occasionally, if we weren't taking the boat out, we'd drive west to the Everglades National Park to fish the canals near Shark Valley. Westchester was centrally located to everything.

If we weren't fishing on Saturday, it was because my dad had to work. Hanging around and watching television or just doing nothing on a non-fishing Saturday, was never an option. After breakfast, my brother and I were told to go find something to do but be back before it got dark. That's when I would cut through yards and jump some fences, so I didn't have to walk around the block to get to my friend's house. We would head up to Westchester Mall, always starting off at Animal Lovers pet store to hold the snakes and play with the puppies before walking around the mall for hours.

Throughout my early childhood years, we belonged to the YM-YWHA, on Eight Street. It had such an impact on me and really made people feel like they belonged to a community. To this day, I'm still friendly with people I met there. It was family oriented, and everybody was friendly. I loved everything about it— especially the snack bar! It had the biggest pool around with low and high diving boards as well as a diving platform which was scary high.

I remember they had family days and for one of their activities, they'd throw coins into the pool and all the kids would go diving down to the bottom to pick up the change.

I was on the swim team for several years and there were always more kids on the team during the summer months than winter months. It was difficult swimming in the winter because the pool wasn't heated. We swam regardless, so after practice I remember rushing to the locker rooms to take a hot shower and not wanting to get out. The swim team is where I met Jacqueline Gutstein and her older brother.

I was involved with everything the club had to offer. I was in judo, tennis, basketball, and softball. I also participated in their summer camps and sports camps.

Once I was in middle school at Rockway Junior High School, I got involved with the YM-YWHA youth groups and was able to get into the teen lounge. What a fun place! During my middle school years, I became addicted to playing pinball. I loved the sound the machines made when the ball hit the bumpers. My friends and I would ride our bikes to Kmart or Zayre just to play pinball in the back. Both stores had that great aroma of popcorn when you entered through the front doors.

When a new pinball arcade opened at the Westchester Mall, I couldn't stay away. Unfortunately, my allowance wasn't enough to pay for my pinball addiction, so I started collecting bottles and mowing lawns. I also got a job washing dishes at China Maid on Bird Road. I remember my dad finding me at the Westchester Mall arcade after school one day, when I should have been home doing my homework and that was the end of my pinball addiction.

Miami Coral Park Senior High was like one big reunion where most of the kids from Banyan, Rockway, Temple Or Olom, and the YM-YWHA ended up together. I followed in my brother's footsteps and got involved with the B'nai B'rith Youth Organization by joining Zion AZA and Topai BBG, which were two Jewish youth groups consisting of mostly Westchester kids.

In high school, it was also important to have a car, so working was mandatory. I worked at Pantry Pride at the Westchester Shopping Center, and at Luria's on Bird Road and Eighty-Seventh Avenue.

Working on my story for this book really helped bring back some great memories that I will be sharing with my wife and kids. It also reminded me of what a great experience it was growing up in Westchester.

Evan Moss

15 | Westchester Schools

I have such wonderful memories of my childhood living and growing up in Westchester. I was fortunate enough to have lived in the same home from the start of my school years to the end of high school. Not many people can say they had the same schoolmates from first through twelfth grade. To witness firsthand, the change in everyone, physically and mentally, was amazing.

Of course, while attending Everglades Elementary School, we all knew who would one day be on the list to become "Most Likely to Succeed" in high school. I remember when homemade cinnamon sticks were being made and sold by students. Some made them so hot that one student suffered a second degree burn from having them in their pocket all day, even though they were wrapped in foil. Remember the Clackers? The heavy, almost golf ball sized balls on the strings that you would make clack up and down. Those were banned because of someone clacking their face. Oh, those fun days!

And then came junior high—or middle school as they call it now. I attended West Miami Junior High School where most of us from Everglades Elementary moved on to. Now there was a whole new clan we'd never met before, not to mention the portable classrooms we'd never seen before. We had a mascot, the Falcon, which was new to us, and our colors–green and gold. This was the time when sports came into the picture for most. New friendships were made, some carrying on through to high school, even if some of them went a different way, to South Miami High School, home of the Cobras. Those of us from Everglades Elementary moved on to the next part of our lives . . . high school.

Oh, boy, do I have great memories of Miami Coral Park Senior High School, and I wouldn't change a thing. That was where I made lifelong friendships, broke swimming records in school, and kicked some butts in water polo (other schools butts)!

And now we had cars! We could leave school and go to lunch, and for those classmates who had a "certain teacher," they may have been asked to leave school—unauthorized—and get doughnuts for those who had the munchies, including the teacher. I heard many stories and witnessed firsthand those that left to purchase doughnuts, because I worked in the Athletics Office for one of my periods, which allowed me to roam the halls at leisure. I just had to avoid being spotted by the assistant principal, Mr. McNulty, who I admired dearly. RIP Mr. McNulty . . . you are truly missed by many.

I had many friends . . . intellectuals, athletes, pranksters (this includes those that let the seventy-nine mice loose at the end of the 1979 school year–you know who you are). I adore them all, even those that hung out in the Dust Bowl. These are the many friends, teachers, and coaches I'll never forget. Many have passed ... some too young and some more recent. RIP my Westchester family. Go Rams!

Robin Lutes Brown-Cilliers

Robin Lutes Brown-Cilliers, 21, at her bachelorette party.

16 | Baby Boomer Paradise

I'm certainly a product of my generation and times. My formative years were the '60s, a time of great uncertainty and grave political threats, yet holding the potential for wonderful societal changes. In my southwest Miami neighborhood of Westchester, just south of the Tamiami Trail, almost as far west as one could be before hitting the Everglades, we thrived, nurtured by our wonderful community.

In 1962, Miami was the target for nuclear missiles aimed from Cuba and where we had sections of Miami Beach closed because our missiles were parked on the beach, pointed back across the water at Cuba. I still have vivid memories of second grade at Everglades Elementary School, participating in a school-wide nuclear missile drill. We had to crouch under our desks, hands over the backs of our heads, and I remember, even at the age of seven or eight, I thought to myself that I might as well kiss my "tush" goodbye, as there was no way this desk would save me from a nuclear missile. But mostly, we felt safe and that we belonged.

When we put aside our existential fears of Russian nuclear annihilation, which we were mostly able to do, our neighborhood in Westchester was a sort of haven, a nurturing world in which to grow up. We often played outside all day long, coming and going in and out of our friends' homes then returning home for dinner.

Everglades Elementary School (home of the Flamingos) was fun. The teachers and principals were smart and caring, and our community seemed to coalesce in support of the school and our neighborhood kids. I sang in the school choir, which often performed a repertoire of old Western songs, and I took ukulele lessons after school from our school's music teacher, a wonderful man who played ukulele and autoharp and taught us Woody Guthrie songs.

We had neighborhood Brownie and Girl Scout troops that met after school, and I remember being especially proud when, on Brownie meeting day, I'd wear my uniform to school, which entitled me to salute the flag rather than put my hand over my heart during our daily Pledge of Allegiance and singing of the Star Spangled Banner. We dutifully brought our quarters to school to fill up the savings bonds books, considered a patriotic duty, and it seemed that everyone participated.

The school librarians were encouraging, and we all read, or at least that's how it seemed. I remember receiving an award for reading all of the biographies in the Everglades Elementary library. One of my classmate's mother, concerned we weren't reading enough, started a junior great books club, to which of course, my parents signed me up.

On Fridays, square dancing replaced regular playground time, and on the days when rockets were launched at Cape Canaveral, we went out on the playground to watch the distant lines and trailing white smoke ascend.

Westchester families, including doctors' and lawyers' families, the families of many small business owners and professionals, as well as those of blue color workers such as plumbers and postmen, lived in fairly similar homes, modest three bedroom, stucco houses they'd purchased in the late '50s and early '60s for, give or take, $12,000. I don't remember class distinctions in our neighborhood, and the majority of families in our part of Westchester were Jewish and very middle class, or so it seemed, and everyone got along. We were the post WWII baby boom, children of patriotic parents who'd lived through the war; many, maybe most, of our fathers had fought in the war.

Miami in the 1960s was our paradise. It was warm almost all the time and we often went barefoot, though we all dressed up for school and social occasions. Nobody locked their doors. When we got older, meaning eight or nine years of age, we walked or rode bikes to the Westchester Shopping Center at the corner of Coral Way and Galloway Road. We took public buses to Coral Gables or elsewhere, staying out for the entire day.

We were within walking distance to Everglades Elementary School, West Miami Junior High, and Miami Coral Park Senior High, as well as to Temple Or Olom and the YM-YWHA, which had purchased a former country club, so it sported an Olympic sized pool, cabanas, tennis and handball courts, a restaurant and snack bar, ballrooms, and more. The YM-YWHA is where most of the Jewish kids went to dances and just hung out in the summers.

Westchester evolved as Cuban immigrants moved in. At Everglades Elementary, we all learned Spanish over the school-wide PA system, broadcast each morning after the school announcements. I remember my parents telling us that the Cubans fit into our neighborhood, because they, like us, valued education and had strong families. In later years, my parents insisted we learn Spanish in school.

Our politics were different though, with Cubans leaning quite a bit to the right wing because of their experiences with the communist takeover in Cuba, whereas most of our family and close friends leaned to the progressive side. I don't remember the circumstances under which I heard of these political differences in our community; mostly, I remember feeling we all belonged.

The biggest trauma of my early Westchester years took place when I was in fourth grade: President John F. Kennedy was assassinated. President Kennedy had articulated our hope and dreams, promoting reading and physical fitness programs to build strong minds and bodies for America's future and, through his ambitious promise to land a "man on the moon" within the next ten years, let us know that even our grandest ambitions were worth pursuing.

We were sent home from school early the day the president was killed, and our parents joined us in the middle of the afternoon. We sat together, stunned, in front of our televisions, hardly believing what our country was experiencing. It was clear that many illusions had been shattered. Our entire community mourned together with our fellow Americans.

As we left the nurturing Everglades Elementary environment for West Miami Junior High and then Miami

Coral Park Senior High, our worlds expanded, becoming a bit less predominantly Jewish and even more diverse. Yet, for whatever reason, our neighborhood schools had still not become racially integrated. Westchester retained the character of a solidly middle class, upwardly mobile community, living the American Dream of that time in history. It seemed that almost all of my classmates at Miami Coral Park High School went to university after high school.

Debbie Dronsky Goldberg (left) and her sister, Robin Dronsky Levine (right), at their Westchester home. Debbie took majorette lessons and performed in the Junior Orange Bowl Parade in Coral Gables.

The Westchester Kids of my generation are the product of our community, of a Miami and an America of the '60s and early '70s. We lived during a time of great hope and promise, when we truly believed society was changing for the better and that huge groups within our country and world would soon be much better off. Many more Americans were prospering economically, the civil rights movement was succeeding, and the women's movement was gaining momentum.

The war in Vietnam would soon end, technology held exciting promises, and we were actually considering the idea of long term peace. We were told we'd soon put humans on the moon, and then we did. We were becoming more and more aware of the need to protect our natural world; we held the first Earth Day celebration and started recycling at the Westchester Shopping Center. And in 1969, girls were finally allowed to wear pants to school!

Debbie Dronsky Goldberg

17 | The Good Ol' Days

The Schwartzman family moved to Westchester at Nineteenth and SW Eighty-Fifth Court in 1964 when I was just three years old and my sister, Paula, was one-year-old. My parents lived in that home until 1992, the year Hurricane Andrew hit South Florida. I have so many fond memories from living in Westchester. The homes on our block were filled with kids all around the same age, and we were always either at each other's homes or outside organizing games.

One of our favorite games to play was street kickball. The wonderful thing about that game was that everyone was invited to play no matter their age. My neighbor, who was a bit older, decided to get some cement and actually build bases around the street. When I went back to visit the neighborhood several years ago, you could still see the worn remnants of the bases he made. We played endless hours outside until our mothers called us in for dinner.

I remember when we were in junior high, my sister, Paula, and her friend Terry wanted to organize a party for the residents of the Coral Gables Convalescent Home located on Eighth Street. So, Paula, twelve, Terry

Adirim, twelve, Terry's sister Joanne, eleven, and friend Stacy Sloan, eleven, planned the event.

They canvassed the neighborhood around Eighty-Fifth Court where we all lived and asked for monetary donations as well as travel-sized soaps, lotions, tissues, and other toiletries. The neighbors were very charitable, and before the girls knew it, they had enough donations to make gift bags for all the residents living at the Convalescent home.

Terry and Paula also wanted to organize some entertainment so they asked me if I would play my clarinet. I was in the West Miami Junior High Band with the late Steve Miranda who also played clarinet. Steve and I played music for the residents, which they enjoyed.

We also sang songs and provided homemade cupcakes and refreshments. As I recall, we didn't get service hours for this project, nor was it a school assignment. It was just a bunch of kids from the old neighborhood getting together to brighten the lives of older Americans. I sometimes compare how we socialized in the 1970s with the way children do so now. Back in the day, I was outside riding my gold banana seat bike, skating with the kind of skates that needed a key, flying kites, playing hopscotch, tag, monkey in the middle, and jacks. The ball was our best friend. Fast forward and most of the socialization opportunities for our kids involved scheduled playdates and activities rather than an impromptu kick ball game. In my current neighborhood, I rarely see kids playing together outside of their homes.

Now that our country is still dealing with the COVID-19 pandemic, kids are being thwarted in their opportunities to socialize with friends even more so. While

I totally agree that we must protect ourselves and our children from this insidious virus, it saddens me to know that these kids are missing out on all of the wonderful experiences I was able to have growing up so many years ago in a quaint Miami suburb called Westchester.

Rhonda Beth Schwartzman Bandes

TIMES/GUIDE   Weekend of May 1/2, 1976

Westchester kids bring Bicentennial to Gables oldsters

A group of Westchester area students has organized a plan to take a bit of the Bicentennial celebration to the residents of Coral Gables Convalescent Home.

Terry Adrion, 12, of 1721 SW 65th Ct., said Friday, April 30, that the six youngsters grouped together and went around their neighborhood collecting presents to take to the elderly residents.

The students, who attend West Miami Junior High and Everglades Elementary, also plan to present Bicentennial entertainment and refreshments. They baked cupcakes, to serve with ice cream, and gathered hand lotion, combs and pocket packets of tissues to give as favors.

Wearing blue jeans and red shirts, the students planned to visit the Home on Saturday, May 1 from 1 to 3 p.m. Those involved, Terry said, include her sister Joanne, 11, Paula Schwartzman, 12, her sister, Rhonda, 14, Stacy Sloan, 10, and Steve Miranda, 14.

Stacy planned to supplement the singing and dancing with a baton exhibition and Rhonda and Steve scheduled clarinet performances.

TIMES/GUIDE May 1/2, 1976

The Times/Guide featured the story of the Westchester kids who visited the Coral Gables Convalescent Home.

Rhonda Beth Schwartzman Bandes (left) and her sister Paula Fine (right) playing their musical instruments.

18 | Moving to "Nowhere"

I'm a Miami native, born in 1951 at St. Francis Hospital on Miami Beach. My dad was in dental school at St. Louis University and my parents came home so I would be born in Miami.

My dad, Jerry Denker, a native of Brooklyn, NY, attended Miami Beach High and played football there in the early 1940s. My grandparents, Julia and Harry Mahler, had a dry cleaning store, DuBarry's, on Fifth Street.

After the war, my dad met my mom, Gloria, from Woodbridge, NJ, while she was vacationing on Miami Beach near the store.

After my dad finished dental school, we moved back to Miami and lived in a small duplex on Southwest Seventh Street in what is now known as Little Havana.

I attended the Miami Jewish Community Center (YM-YWHA), also located in the neighborhood, for kindergarten.

In 1955, we moved to a new housing development called Westchester. Everyone wondered why we were moving to "nowhere" in the Everglades. Actually, it was in the area of Coral Way between Southwest Seventy-Eighth and Eighty-Seventh Avenues. There were no expressways, and the neighborhood was barren at first, with no trees or landscaping. My father set up his dental practice on Bird Road and I attended Everglades Elementary School.

In 1957, when I was seven, my sister, Marti, was born at Jackson Memorial Hospital. Little did I know that as an adult, I would work at Jackson as a nurse for more than thirty-eight years.

Westchester was a great neighborhood for growing up. We played ball games, rode bikes on the quiet streets, and knew most everyone in the community.

My dad, a proud Gator from the University of Florida, influenced my sister and me in many ways. Dad was an all-time sports lover, and we spent much time at the Orange Bowl, cheering on the University of Miami Hurricanes, claiming season tickets when the Dolphins arrived in Miami, attending the Golden Gloves boxing in Dinner Key, and any other sporting event that came to town.

I have many remembrances of the "sleepy" town in Miami where we didn't lock our homes or cars. We picked strawberries and tomatoes blocks from our home. We walked to the shopping center in Westchester and bought 45 rpm records at Zayre store. I spent summers hanging out with friends and club members at the Westbrook Country Club on Southwest Eighth Street, later to become the YM-YWHA where my Coral Park swim team practiced. My family liked to go out to eat and some of our favorites were the Red Diamond on Lejeune, the Pub, and Glorified Deli on Coral Way.

My grandparents lived on Miami Beach, and it was always a treat to sleep over and go to Flamingo Park and the beach. I remember the long ride to the beach weaving in and out of streets through downtown before the expressways were built. My girlfriends and I would sometimes take the bus to South Beach and hang out by the old dog track.

If it wasn't the beach, we'd ride the bus to Miracle Mile, shop at Young Sophisticates, eat lunch at Jahn's Ice Cream Parlor, and see a movie at the Miracle Theatre.

As a result of the sports culture in our lives, I became a competitive swimmer and swam with the Coral Gables Swimming Association at the Venetian pool from 1959 until I joined the Miami Coral Park Senior High School swimming team in 1966. My sister became a competitive tennis player and often played at Salvador Park in Coral Gables.

My mom, very dedicated, would drive us back and forth to swimming or tennis practice, sometimes more than twice a day. We'd spend weekends at swimming meets anywhere from Miami to West Palm Beach.

To this day, I continue to swim and work out with groups at José Martí Park. I have great friends from my age-group swimmers and the Masters swimming community of South Florida.

Needless to say, I attended the University of Florida and also became a loyal Gator and a nurse practitioner. I spent a great thirty-eight years at Jackson Memorial Hospital in many roles, caring for the people of Miami-Dade County. I continue to reside in Miami in a building with a great view of the beautiful bay and downtown skyline, not far from the little duplex that still stands on Southwest Seventh Street.

Ann-Lynn Denker
Courtesy of HistoryMiami Museum's Miami Stories initiative

Ann-Lynn Denker at her Westchester home.

19 | Westchester Was Special

Fleeing communism, my family moved from Cuba to Mexico, and finally to Westchester in 1968 when I was eight years old. We moved to Miami because we had family here, it was reasonably priced, and the warm weather reminded us of Cuba, our homeland.

Back in the '60s, Westchester was considered to be so far away from the middle of Miami that people would ask "You live way out there?" Our neighbors were great people with strong family foundations, and there was little to no crime that I was aware of. There were a lot of kids in our neighborhood, and we'd play outside until the sun went down.

I remember shopping at Zayre and JByrons and going to eat pancakes at IHOP, and Cuban food at Lila's Restaurant and Rio Crystal. My parents would take us to Westward Ho! once a month as a special treat.

I attended Coral Park Elementary and remember some teachers were perplexed because I didn't understand English, having arrived in Miami from Mexico where I spoke only Spanish in my early childhood. I wasn't thrilled with school, but I loved my art class and playing sports. I remember receiving seven presidential awards while I attended Coral Park. After elementary, I attended Rockway Junior High School where I had three wonderful teachers, Ms. Lopez, Ms. Mathews and my Spanish teacher, Mrs. Nodarse. At Rockway, I especially enjoyed art class and PE. I met a lot of friends at that school, and

Vivian Sanchez-Villalba and her mother, Myriam.

my mom and another parent would take turns driving us and some neighbors to school. For some reason, I didn't do after school activities while in junior high. I went on to attend and graduate from Miami Coral Park Senior High

School and fondly remember Miss Fran King, our volleyball coach. She was great with us, and I learned a lot from her. I also played soccer, and sports meant the world to me. Our house was two blocks from the high school, so we'd walk to school.

I still have so many great friends I made at the schools I attended, and we still connect either in person or on social media, even after fifty-five years! We still get together with a group of girlfriends from my childhood and teen years a couple of times a year and have lunch and reminisce.

When I think of Westchester, I think of a life filled with simplicity, honesty, and so many good times. I thank my parents for moving our family to Westchester, because it gave me and my sister the best childhood a kid could ask for, and it made me a better person with good values.

Vivian Sanchez-Villalba

20 | Blue Light Special

Two-year-old Cristy Justo stands in front of her father's "pisicorre" at her house near Bird Bowl.

Growing up in Westchester, we went on a shopping trip every weekend to our neighborhood Kmart and Westchester Mall on SW Eighty-Seventh Avenue and Coral Way. For a Hispanic family adapting to a new life in the U.S., this was a fun trip and we spent at least two hours inside Kmart. Two hours of going up and down every single aisle looking at things I could only wish to bring home.

At Kmart, it felt like a stage production, with an intermission for lunch at their cafeteria in the very back of the store. They had the best roast beef, mashed potatoes, and apple cobbler ever! This was my only break from eating Cuban food daily. Regarding the food at Kmart, my mom would say in her native Spanish, *"Niña, eso no es comida."* Translation, "Girl, that isn't food." It was honestly the highlight of my week as a kid.

I explored the store with my fingers crossed to hear the famous "Blue Light Special" store announcement for subs, or as my mom called them, *submarinos*. That announcement, combined with the bright blue siren, would mean I got one for dinner. For me, that was a total score!

Finally, we'd make a stop at the churro man's cart who occupied the first parking space right outside the front doors of the store. That sweet old man made the most delicious and freshest churros in Westchester. They were truly the best I've ever had. I'd stand there with a giant smile and the old man would throw in extra pieces for me coated with sugar. That white, greasy paper bag filled with churros made so many kids happy. I guess you can say this Latin girl loved American food and some good traditional Latin treats like churros as well.

My memories of what I like to call "Old Florida Westchester" will always live in my heart!

Cristy Justo

21 | The Best Place to Grow Up

Growing up in Westchester in the 1970s was wonderful. We had great weather, great friends, good music, and innocent fun. My parents bought a house in Westchester in anticipation of my birth in Miami in 1961. We lived in that house when my two sisters were born and didn't leave the area until I was seventeen when we moved to Arizona.

In Westchester, all the neighborhood children were friends with each other, and our parents were all friendly with one another as well. We didn't have cliques and we all got along.

I attended Everglades Elementary School where the teachers cared about us and our education. I remember my teachers, Mrs. Fisher, Mrs. Howell, Mrs. Shaw, Mrs. Joffee, Mrs. Brookman, Mr. McCluskey, and Mrs. Sager. Everglades didn't have air conditioning, except for third grade, which was very exciting. We buried time capsules in the back field of the school, and I still wonder if anyone ever found them.

On weekends and after school, we rode bikes to our friends' houses and played outside, games like jacks and hopscotch, among others. On rainy days, we played board games inside and my favorite was Go to the Head of the Class. My friend Lori Zalis had that game, and I always wanted to play it when I went to her house. I remember going to my friend Anne Randall's house, with my Barbie dolls and we played with them for hours on end. I also played basketball at the school playground on weekends. Although we didn't have cell phones back then, we knew we had to be home by dark.

Suzanne Schweitzer Shlian, 9, dressed in a Halloween costume in 1969 inside her Westchester home.

After I graduated from Everglades, I attended West Miami Junior High. There was no air conditioning in that school either, but we survived. By the time I was in junior high, I was allowed to walk to the Westchester Shopping Center from my house and I would window shop, go to the movies with my friends, and of course, always made a stop at Mister Donut.

After junior high, I attended Miami Coral Park Senior High School and went to football games, went bowling, attended the Youth Fair on Coral Way, hung out at Burger King, and went to the beach with my friend Susie Podel. We took two buses to get to the beach and we always had fun watching the surfer dudes and getting tanned. I also took the bus from Florida International University to go to the Orange Bowl Stadium to see the Miami Dolphins play football.

I went with my friends to Temple Or Olom on the high holidays and some Shabbats. Sometimes, my mom would drop me off at Bird Bowl or Sunland Roller Skating rink on a hot afternoon. On Sundays, my parents would take us to Miami Beach, and that was always a fun day.

My dad's favorite restaurant in Westchester, and where we ate all the time, was Lum's. Other times my mom would order Chinese take-out for many dinners, but since I didn't like the food, she would get my dinner from Burger King. The public library had a traveling bookmobile that came to Westchester Shopping Center once a week and I looked forward to checking out books. A carnival came to Westchester once a year and that was always fun to go to. Those were some of the highlights of living in Westchester. We had the YM-YWHA close to our house and I enjoyed swimming there and took lifesaving classes and art classes. During the summer, I went to day camp at the club and I remember the trampoline was my favorite part of camp.

Westchester was the best place to grow up. I had the best of times with lots of wonderful memories and I'm thankful I had that opportunity.

Suzanne Schweitzer Shlian

22 | New Home, New Life in Westchester

My mother had become a widow after my father, Mingo Trueba, had been executed by a firing squad for his participation as the point man for the CIA's invasion of the Bay of Pigs in Cuba. We'd been living in a rental house near the airport for five years when my brothers met their friend Billy at the canal on Sixty-Second Avenue and Blue Lagoon. His mother, Emily, mentioned to my mother about the new neighborhood she was moving to. So, my mom went to check out the area at the end of Tamiami Trail, Eighth Street and Ninety-Seventh Avenue, where Coral Park Elementary School, Rockway Junior High, and Miami Coral Park Senior High were all within walking distance. This was a convenient option that enabled us kids to walk to school, allowing her one less chore so she could drive to work at Modernage Furniture store in Coral Gables. There she worked as a receptionist and then became the first saleswoman for the store located on Miracle Mile.

It was the beginning of June 1966 when my mother Marta, her mother Lola, and the four of us kids, Domingo,

Jose, Elena, and myself, moved to the house on Sixteenth Street. We were lucky enough to have found this house, and with a gift from my aunt and uncle who gave the $1,000 dollar deposit, my mother took over the payments from the bank. Back in 1962, this type of four bedroom home with a full size pool was being built for around $25,000 in Westchester.

We were thrilled to spend the entire day in the pool while our abuela took care of us, cooking and controlling us kids who were jumping in the canal in back of the house and swimming to the bridge on Ninety-Seventh Avenue. After that summer, we started school and I was to spend my last year in sixth grade at Coral Park. I always wore a dress and little white girly socks, and while I was not the shy type, this was a whole new change for me.

The kids were very modern and cool Americans, so I didn't think I'd be able to fit in. I don't know if Billy, who was in my grade, gave the heads-up or if it was just the kindness of the coolest chick at school, Andrea, but she knew everyone and she came up to me with a welcome that until this day, I have never forgotten. She was friends with so many people.

Andrea and I had invented a certain call we would yell across from the back of the canal from the back yard of her house on Fifteenth Street to mine on Sixteenth Street. One day I was even invited to a fancy Bar Mitzvah for my friend Michael along with all of our other friends. It was the first party I attended that seemed like a grown-up style bash!

It was the late 1960s, the British invasion was in full swing, and Twiggy became a supermodel. In 1967, Andrea was the first to get the Twiggy style haircut. I had to cry and beg for my mother to agree for me to get the same haircut so that I could follow the trend.

At the end of the school year, our sixth grade graduation took place. We all wore the flowered mini dresses, fish net stockings, and our first makeup including lipstick, foundation, and wild eyeliner.

I am so happy to have been a part of this very special time in the history of the Westchester area, when we didn't have a care in the world.

Back then almost anything west of Ninety-Seventh Avenue was cow pasture, along with the Tamiami Airport that is now the grounds of Florida International University.

I remember a friend of ours had a horse at the pasture where the Publix Shopping Center is now on 107th Avenue, and her, Andrea and myself went over to check it out. With the help of the girls, they lifted me onto the horse bareback and it took off, throwing me to the ground. My friends were both in stitches, and I was in shock, although unhurt.

We were daring kids back then, getting on the bus at Sixteenth Street and Ninety-Seventh Avenue, taking it to the Coral Gables station, then transferring to the downtown line, and on to South Beach on Saturdays, bikinis in tow.

The pier was a popular spot to watch the kids jump into the water and the surfers do their thing. The Dog Racing Track was at the south point with the jetty, the Coast Guard Station, and a parking lot facing the beach. On Ocean Drive the Bagel Guy would sell thirteen bagels for a dollar back then, this was way before Nikki Beach.

In the winter, we'd take the bus to Coral Gables and just walk around Miracle Mile, and for lunch, we'd eat at Jahn's, Denny's, or Burger King and maybe catch a movie at the Miracle Theatre that's still there. Once Dadeland Mall opened up, it became our new stomping ground.

In 1967, we went off to Rockway Junior High School, which was a much bigger school, so it was a good thing many of us knew each other already. We had the Falcons football team, chorus, Coach Solinger, Spanish class, and science class that showed us films about frogs and other creatures. There was no air conditioning back in the day and most of us would nap during the movies.

The coolest guy in school was Roger with his black, long and beautiful straight hair. He was an eighth grader, and the girls would swoon every time he walked by.

The students from the Miccosukee Tribe that attended Rockway lived on their Reservation off Tamiami Trail in the Everglades out west and my brother Domingo was friends with many of them because he would go fishing out there.

The best times were the Friday night dances in the cafeteria where one popular kid, Roy, had a line of girls waiting to slow dance with him. We eventually got into spin the bottle parties where we got to kiss the boys, many of us for the first time! After school, our group would walk to the Corral restaurant at the Westchester Shopping Center to hang out.

We'd walk to Rockway Junior High along Ninety-Seventh Avenue where all the cow pastures were, and it seemed the end of the world was just west of there—the Everglades.

Little by little more construction began, and brand new homes were being built all the way to 107th Avenue. From Bird Road to the Trail, the streets were lined with huge pine trees all the way to Krome Avenue near the Pit Bar-B-Q restaurant that is still there today. Westchester had grown so much in the 1960s and many more Cuban

Photo credit: Andrea Rosenfeld Cote'

Martica D. Trueba during her years at
Rockway Junior High School.

immigrants had moved to the area. Everyone got along great, and those days were awesome.

Times and music were changing as Janis Joplin and Jimi Hendrix were famous, both performing in Miami, as well as The Doors in Coconut Grove. Jim Morrison had gotten arrested for pulling his pants down in front of the crowd. Hendrix, Alice Cooper, Sly and the Family Stone and many local bands played at the Miami Jai-Alai. But the biggest event of all was Joplin performing in 1969 at an outdoor concert where the Big Five Club is today.

I was fourteen years old then and there was no way I would have ever been allowed at a psychedelic concert where people were smoking pot and free love was happening. Now, I think to myself, I should have crossed Eighth Street (Tamiami Trail) up that scary dirt road and just tried to get in for free!

We graduated ninth grade and went on to Miami Coral Park Senior High School on Sixteenth Street and Eighty-Eighth Avenue. The school was just five years old with an auditorium, gymnasium, wood shop, printing and camera class, biology, tennis, football, baseball, and drama class. It was sensational.

I got into gymnastics, but quickly changed to modern dance. I remember one of my friends, Mari, who was in gymnastics at the time and a brilliant athlete, passed away suddenly after graduation. She was funny and beautiful—a very special angel. During the middle of tenth grade, in 1970, the principal made an announcement that would change our lives forever as well as the course of history. Girls were allowed to wear pants to school! Out with the dresses and skirts, and in with the bell bottomed jeans as all hell broke loose.

The guys had afros and long hair and we wore tie dye T-shirts and tennis shoes, now known as sneakers! Coach Solinger had followed us from Rockway to become the biology teacher. Miss Fran King, whom I knew from the Allapattah YMCA, was the gymnastics teacher and cheerleading coach for us Rams. We had art class, creative writing, and fun rallies in the gym.

Another girl and I were the only girls in our printing class, and it seemed sex was always the topic of conversation in the dark room. The best class of all was Drivers Education that was held in the parking lot of the school. All of the kids would hit the orange cones and we would laugh our butts off.

The Vietnam War was taking place back then and many of our friends' older brothers had been drafted into that terrible war.

There were so many of us in the old gang, too many to mention them all, but we had at least two who became movie stars like Steven Bauer and Andy Garcia. The beautiful Carol who would go on to marry my lucky brother Jose was part of our group. Adal is remembered for always carrying his fringe satchel. Ali was the artist in our group, the rock star Ish, and the swim team. I remember all of them fondly. They are, and will always be, my Westchester peeps.

Martica D. Trueba

23 | Part-Time Westchester Girl

Growing up on a part-time basis in Westchester was great. I lived farther east in the Shenandoah neighborhood and went every weekend to visit my cousin, Robin Lutes, who is the same age as I am. Robin who is green eyed and me with brown eyes sported the same outfits and the Buster Brown haircuts.

I spent many summer weekends playing with Barbies and Robin had a collection of small toy horses which were always included with the dolls.

Our favorite pastime was goofing around outdoors, because there were many other children in the neighborhood to hang out with. We swam in the pool, played hopscotch, rode bikes, and roller skated.

Westchester seemed so far away that it was like being on vacation. All our cousins gathered at Robin's house in Westchester because it was quite the happening place at the time.

One thing she had that I didn't in my neighborhood was the woods. Her back yard was Tamiami Trail, Eighth Street, and from the Palmetto Expressway to Eighty-Seventh Avenue, it was all woods. Today it has strip malls and businesses all along Tamiami

Trail. We had many adventures in those woods, from scavenger hunts and trail walks to teenagers just snooping around, performing small burials for dead birds and rabbits along the way.

Across the Trail were the canals and, to us, it was exciting to cross over and go fishing. My older brother, sister, and I, would catch the bus from our Shenandoah neighborhood to go fishing at the canals. My mother would later find out and be so mad we'd traveled that far alone. After our fishing trips we would cross over to our Aunt Gracie's house (Robin's home) to get fed and we got back on the #5 bus for our long travel home. Back in those days we were expected to be home by dark.

We also frequented the Gooney Golf, located on Tamiami Trail and I remember those golfing adventures where I'd cheat and crawl under the windmill to put my ball in the hole. We'd go to the Westchester Shopping Center and buy our toys at Lionel Playworld, which was a treat, and I only made a few visits to the movie theater. At the Westchester Mall we'd go to JByrons which was the place to shop for our clothes.

As I got older, I wanted a horse like Robin and her sisters had, and one summer they bought me one. His name was Splotch, a big, hefty Pinto. We kept it at the B BAR B Ranch right behind the Big Five Club. I was supposed to take the bus daily to feed and groom my horse, but as kids are, and being very irresponsible at age twelve, the horse was soon sold, and I lost that opportunity.

When I reached high school, I was not doing very well with my grades. I was attending Miami Senior High and failing rapidly. My father was irate. I grew up in a very lenient household with my parents, grandparents, aunts, uncles, and siblings. It was a free-for-all. When your parents said no, you would run to your grandparents for the yes! My father gave me the option to either go to an all-girl Catholic school or move to Westchester to live with my cousin Robin and attend Miami Coral Park Senior High.

Katherine M. Fuller in her teenage years in the late '70s.

I opted for the latter thinking it was going to be a better deal. Little did I know that there were rules and curfews. I got to Coral Park in the last semester of the tenth grade in 1977.

Our Coral Park basketball games were always fun and after the games we'd all gather and have pizza on Bird

Road and Eighty-Seventh Avenue. Robin and I also went to many Coral Park house parties with our friends and my last year at Coral Park we'd sneak out of school and go to the McDonald's on Ninety-Seventh Avenue for lunch.

I wasn't allowed out on school nights unless there was a school game. Dinner was at 6 p.m. sharp and the weekend curfew was midnight; I'd never had that kind of structure before. I graduated high school in 1979 along with all my peers, thanks to my cousin Robin and her family who made it all possible.

I'm still very close with Robin, but her family home is no longer in Westchester. My aunts and uncles have passed, and Robin now resides in northern Florida. I still live in my childhood home in the Shenandoah neighborhood.

My memories of Westchester are great and are still in my heart because it was my adopted neighborhood growing up.

Katherine M. Fuller

24 | A Gringa in Westchester

People always asked me and still do, "Where were you born?" When I tell them I was born in Doctors Hospital in Coral Gables they're shocked because most people have transplanted here from New York or New Jersey. I'm proud I can say I'm a Native Floridian.

I only moved from my house at Thirty-Third Terrace and Seventy-Ninth Avenue twice in my fifty-eight years, once to Whisperwood (1995 to 1996), an apartment complex next to Baptist Hospital, and to Thornton, Colorado (1996 to 1998). The rest of the time I spent in my childhood home.

I had my best friend who lived next door whose mom was Puerto Rican, and her dad was from Cuba. My mom and my grandmother were always invited over for family gatherings, and to this day, I still keep in touch with all of them.

I learned Spanish since some of them, including my friend's abuelo, only spoke a few words of English, and, of course, I learned the bad words first. It was useful to learn the Spanish cuss words because if I stubbed my toe or something bad happened, I could say *coño* instead of saying an English cuss word and it was awesome since my mom and grandmother didn't understand what I was saying. I also remember going to Lila's Restaurant and getting the *papitas con bistec. ¡Que rico!*

I fondly remember the wonderful teachers at Emerson Elementary, and it's especially funny that years later, my son who is now twenty-five years old, had some of the same teachers I had. Back then, we all considered anyone over thirty a dinosaur.

I remember the barrels we had on the field and hiding in them, and now thinking about how nasty they were inside, I can't believe I did that. I believe the school put them there as inexpensive props for the kids to play with. I wish I'd gotten a picture of them as they as they are no longer there.

I lived two blocks away from Emerson, so my grandmother used to walk me to school until I got older, then I'd walk with friends instead.

One of my favorite things in PE was Field Day. I remember passing the baton, square dancing, gymnastics, and the worst activity we did was hanging from the monkey bars. I dreaded picture day as I always seemed to get a fever blister just in time, and with my starched dress and hair stiff from hairspray, I just wanted to get it over with.

I remember the cafeteria and the smell of green beans and carrots, and especially the wild food fights which occurred every once in a while. Although I didn't like math, English and history were my favorite subjects because I excelled in them.

There was a farm down the street from Emerson, and I used to go and watch the horses running around there. They seemed so happy. I usually take an evening walk around the neighborhood, and I see a lot of changes everywhere, especially when I see the houses where my peers used to live.

I have so many memories of working at the Tropicaire Drive-In Theatre and Flea Market. I worked there from 1980 to 1985 while attending Miami Dade College Kendall Campus. It was my first "real" job, which I got, in part, because of a family friend's granddaughter who was working there during her summer vacation. She was visiting here from California, and when she left, she recommended me to the boss and assistant manager at the time.

At Tropicaire Drive-In, I worked in the concession stand/snack bar, Thursday through Sunday night for the movies, and Saturday and Sunday for the Flea Market, later becoming the assistant manager of the concession stand at night for the movies.

I remember the people coming in to try to steal candy, especially Twizzlers (yuck), while I was making the fresh popcorn. Most people wanted lots of butter on their popcorn, or as it we called it, suntan oil, because it was nasty, but they wanted their grease. During the sweltering summer days, when I had to run to the back to cook the hot dogs, I'd go into the walk-in freezer to cool off. It was kind of strange, because when we were young and running around doing stuff outdoors, the heat didn't bother us as much as it does now.

I used to give away ice even though we were supposed to charge for it, but being kids, we didn't charge, and we got a lot of good stuff or discounts in return, especially rock 'n' roll T-shirts, hair stuff, etcetera. During the night shift at the movies, we used to laugh at the back row of cars, because we knew why they'd park there. "If this van's a rockin', don't come a knockin'!" The security guys used to go around and flash their light in their cars just to annoy the people. A good thing about working there was that I lived six blocks away, so when I pulled a double shift on weekends, I had time to nap for a couple of hours before getting ready for the night crowd.

I was also taking classes in Travel and Tourism because I wanted to work for the airlines or at a travel agency. But my grandmother always loved Baptist Hospital, and I eventually went there to interview and

*Wendy Marie Welch with her beloved dog, Laddie,
who enjoyed goofing around with her.*

began to work as a file clerk. Now after thirty-five years I'm currently an Appeals and Denial Specialist in the same department I started at, just a different job position, and one of the guys that I met back then is now a CEO of

Finance at Baptist Hospital. When I saw him again, we had some good laughs over those days.

I've grown up with some people from my childhood, and still see them, but lost touch with others. Then suddenly they show up where you work or you run into them around town and I still chat online with my peeps from those days on social media. I met a lot of people from all walks of life, and it's really cool to see the direction everyone's lives have taken.

I have good memories of those days growing up in Westchester and of our simple way of life back then.

Wendy Marie Welch

25 | A Nerd No More

In 1959, my parents bought their newly built house in Westchester. The neighborhood ended up having a lot of Jewish families, and my parents made friends at the YM-YWHA on SW Eighth Street, Temple Or Olom on SW Sixteenth Street, and local Jewish organizations such as Hadassah and the Knights of Pythias.

There were many Jewish families with children in the area who all grew up together, sharing experiences at Everglades Elementary, West Miami Junior High, and Miami Coral Park Senior High, as well as at summer camps at the YM-YWHA and religious school at Temple Or Olom.

As time went on, more Cuban families moved into Westchester, and many of the Jewish families migrated out of the area once their children graduated high school.

I was one of the nerds. I was good at math and the person that was most inspiring to me was John Hazleton, a black teacher at West Miami Junior High who was also a guidance counselor. He recognized my math skills, letting me know that it was okay to be smart.

Being in the Miami-Dade County Public School System, I was able to be in the Deep Accelerated Math

Program, where I could take college math courses while in high school, which allowed me to accelerate my education in college and graduate school, where I earned a PhD.

There was a price to pay for being a nerd. It was a social challenge, because it was hard to be one of the more popular kids. Now that I've reconnected with many high school friends and acquaintances, mostly through social media, the social challenge has disappeared, and it seems that more people have respect for the work I did back then that made me the nerd I was.

Irvin Lustig, 13, stands outside the Miss Florida yacht
where he held his Bar Mitzvah reception.

There was another benefit in growing up in an area with people from different cultural, religious, and even socio-economic backgrounds, with a variety of skills across many different areas. Not everyone was book-smart with good grades, but everyone had their own special talent.

The interactions I had with them prepared me to communicate and interact with people later in my life. At Brown, where I went to college, I met people who'd gone to private prep schools who didn't know how to have a simple conversation with a variety of people.

Growing up in Westchester taught me how to acquire that valuable life skill of how to build relationships with people coming from all walks of life.

Irvin Lustig

26 | For the Love of Teaching

My parents and family lived in upstate New York in the mountains, owning a general store and luncheonette for years. The main road that led to their general store was going to be demolished to make room for a highway.

That was disastrous for my family, but realizing no one would buy the land, they closed up the store and gave it to the fire department to use as a practice house to burn, demolish, etcetera.

They packed up all our belongings and we left for Florida where it was warmer. My mom suffered from arthritis, so warm climates, wooden floors, and the beach was what she needed. They moved in 1958, and I was born a year later in 1959.

For the next thirteen years, we called Westchester home. In the community, my dad owned two gas stations, one on Eighth Street and one off the Palmetto across from West Miami Junior High School. There was a small bike store across the street that had candy, so we frequented this shop often as well as other small businesses that lined the main streets of Westchester.

My home was wonderful, and I have so many great memories from the time I lived there. We had a huge tree in the front yard that we all used to climb and a big yard to play hide and seek in. Our property had numerous fruit trees that provided snacks for us, and my dad built me a playhouse the size of a school portable, furniture and all, that we had many years of enjoyment playing in, and had sleep overs too.

During my childhood and early teens, I learned to play piano, and enjoyed ballet, tap, jazz, gymnastics, ceramics classes, and attended the Art Linkletter Dance Studio for many years, loving the recitals and meeting many friends.

My old neighborhood on Eighty-Second Avenue had a variety of families and lots of kids. The grandma across the street used to bake bread and lay it out on her front porch, where the smell radiated throughout the street. I always got a loaf, yum. The man next door played trumpet at the Castaways Hotel and Bar at night and then came home and rehearsed until the wee hours of the morning.

A pilot for Eastern Airlines lived behind us, and about three years ago, his daughter Nancy and I came across each other on social media. It had been quite a few years, but it was good to reconnect. I attended Everglades Elementary School in Westchester, which back then included grades first through sixth, and we either walked to school or our parents drove us. We had small classrooms with windows but no air conditioning.

Portables didn't exist then, and the school had no surrounding fences. We carried lunch boxes to school and dressed up for picture day. Everglades Elementary instilled great social and learning skills in me at a young age.

As for me, I really enjoyed going to school, and I liked and admired my teachers. For my ninth birthday, I asked for and received a double sided chalk board, green on one side, black on the other, and had colored chalk! After school almost every day, my friends and I would play "school" and do our homework too. All my friends told me they knew I'd make a great teacher someday.

The only teacher I can't remember is from fourth grade, but I fondly remember Mrs. Fisher, Mrs. Sager, and Mrs. Fund. I knew then that I wanted to be a teacher when I grew up and I did! In fifth grade, I remember I had Camille King, and I remember her because that year we had Hurricane Camille, and lastly, I recall Ms. Parks. Thank you to all the teachers, staff, and the great friends I made and still keep in touch with over fifty years later.

We moved to Ft. Lauderdale when I was thirteen, and I was homesick. It was a tough year, but I made friends, got involved in school and music, and I still talk to quite a few friends from Miami.

I've seen some of them and traveled back to show my sons where I spent my childhood, and yes, the Westchester area and Everglades Elementary School too. I really enjoyed growing up there and it was a special time.

All those great experiences molded me into a great adult, a loving mom of two wonderful sons, and a teacher for over thirty-two years. The majority of my teaching was in grades five and six, maybe because I thought I had something to prove since sixth grade wasn't as enjoyable to me because of the teacher I had. Oddly enough, they were my favorite years to teach, and I ended up teaching third grade during my last year. So, a big thank you goes out for my time of learning, growing, and developing great skills and friendships from Everglades Elementary School.

I currently live near the beach in Sarasota, but my memories of Westchester will always stay dear to my heart.

Ruthann Paul-Suess

Ruthann Paul-Suess during her last year of teaching after thirty-two years.

27 | Westchester Girl at Heart

I have many Westchester memories and some of my favorites took place with friends and in school. At the time, I lived in the apartment complex called Green Briar

West on Ninety-Sixth Avenue and Coral Way.

I attended Olympia Heights Elementary School and that's when I began singing and joined choir for the first time. This was a pivotal time for me as it kick-started my passion for music. One of the most impactful memories I have is performing with the Olympia Heights choir for Mayor Alex Penelas.

Lilymar Montenegro

I'm proud to have been a part of that monumental event. We sang a piece called *It's My Journey*, which was taught to us by our choir teacher, Mr. Abril. He influenced me in many positive ways. He'd always make us work hard, but he did so because he cared deeply and knew we were capable of absolute excellence, and he was right. We were an outstanding choir group thanks to him.

When my mother told me one day we were moving to Texas, I was so bummed, mostly because in addition to dance, I was also part of the choir at my high school, and it was something that I'd been doing since I was younger at Olympia Heights. The reason it was so significant to me was because after three years of auditioning, I'd finally made it to the vocals choir team. It was a choir group of advanced singers that required a successful audition to be chosen for the team and the move meant that I would have to start over in Texas.

I eventually moved, continued high school as a junior, and joined the choir at my new school in Houston. It was a difficult transition because I experienced intense culture shock upon arriving in Texas. Over time I adjusted and have lived there ever since.

While living in Westchester, I enjoyed going to the Xtra and Winn-Dixie grocery stores with my grandmother and stopping at a local Cuban bakery for *pastelitos* on the way there. I still remember my grandmother driving to the craft store, Diamonds, to buy materials and fabric to sew with, and First Union Bank where she had her account.

I was there when Ferguson High School was still being built, and we hosted many of their students at Braddock High during the construction. I made a lot of friends from Ferguson, and although there was some tension at first, we eventually all got along, and the Braddock students were sad to see them leave once their school was finished.

I also miss taking the private buses home after school that my family paid for. I rode one with a lovely lady bus driver that I'll never forget. She was always so sweet and accommodating and would wait a bit for some of the children if they were running a few minutes late. She even allowed us to store shaving cream bottles in her bus for the shaving cream celebrations that took place on the last day of school.

The principal would prohibit us from bringing backpacks on the last day of school to avoid those celebrations, but students would find clever ways of hiding them around the building or even in the bushes. I wonder if those shaving cream celebrations still take place.

During my time living at Green Briar West apartments, I spent a lot of time playing outside with neighborhood kids. I met two girls who became my best friends at that time. We'd ride bikes around the complex, climb trees, sing, and create dance routines. This was a very memorable time for me and one of those girls is still my best friend today. Ironically, she moved to Texas for a year in 2015, and we reconnected again. We'd lost touch after middle school because she'd moved away from the apartment complex.

There was also a boy in my neighborhood who'd ride his bike outside by my room. We'd chat through the open window and sometimes ride our bikes together. I knew he liked me, but he never knew that I had a crush on him as well.

I now go back to visit my family in Miami at least once a year. My dad and cousins still live there as well as a few of my friends with whom I keep in close contact with. I make it a point to drive by my elementary, middle, and high school once in a while when I visit. I also went back to Green Briar West, and I was surprised to see how little it had changed.

All of my childhood memories came flooding back the last time I visited. I experienced an abundance of fun recollections, including shenanigans such as skipping class to go spend the day at the beach (and my mother wondered why I was so tanned, lol), my first kiss, my first boyfriend, and my first heartbreak, all in Westchester.

Although I've lived in Texas for the last sixteen years, I'll always be a true Westchester girl at heart. That will forever be my home and where a piece of my heart will always remain.

Lilymar Montenegro

28 | Zayre: A Second Home

I lived just behind Zayre in Westchester and we made regular trips there with my mom starting when I was in a stroller. As a toddler, I made some rookie errors like stealing a cowboy hat and breaking some mirrors, but all in all, pretty harmless stuff.

When I got my first bicycle, I could venture to Zayre on my own or with a friend, so at least twice a week, my best friend, Rosemary, and I would ride our bikes there with pocket money to spend.

The first stop was always the record section, looking at the LPs and 45s. I recall 45s were ninety-nine cents back then. Then a trip to the toy section before heading to the back of the store where we would get a hot dog or slice of pizza at the snack bar and play pinball for hours, or so it seemed. Zayre was a place where you always felt safe and welcome, and the staff treated us like family.

In the summertime, Zayre was a place where you hung out to stay cool and in the winter, near Christmas, where people from the Salvation Army were ringing their bells and looking for donations. The store was very connected to our community.

I think the turning point for Zayre came when Lionel Playworld opened in the shopping center on the other side of Galloway Road. Toys in absolute mass! Aisles and aisles of everything from sporting goods to Barbies.

Soon after, a third shopping center emerged that had JC Penney and an indoor mall full of small specialty shops. Zayre had monopolized the area for so long, but by the early '70s, the face of Westchester had changed to meet the needs of its growing Hispanic population, and customer loyalty had shifted. I watched many of the old

Donna Rose (left) with her Westchester childhood friend Rosemary Rubino Hartenhoff (right).

familiar stores and restaurants close, but I knew in my heart, those childhood memories would always remain.

A Party to Remember

This is kind of a parallel story to the party at Joel's in Risky Business, except for the fact it occurred five years earlier in the sedate neighborhood of Westchester, and we didn't put a car in the water.

I was in the tenth grade attending Miami Coral Park Senior High School at the time and my friend's parties were a tradition that began in 1976. When their parents took a long vacation, their housekeeper was left to supervise them, but we were able to distract her, and the party goers started drifting in.

We were all feeling pretty good by the early evening and the party was well and truly underway. The kegs were flowing, blenders going, pool was full, music was on loop, the bedrooms were busy, but all in all, pretty tame by today's standards, or so it seemed.

As the night progressed, more people started to arrive, and it got crazy. Some football players came in with copious quantities of beer and their unique brand of drunken charm. The palm tree in the front yard soon became a catapult with guys being flung over parked cars in the street, and with one guy leaping from the roof onto the palm, snapping it in half. Apparently when the kegs dried up, some people made their way into the family stash of vintage wine and opened most of it, chugging down expensive bottles of red.

The next day, there were people asleep everywhere in the house, the palm tree was dead, cars were damaged, and empty bottles of liquor were floating in the pool.

Friends continued to come and go over those three weeks, but my friends were grounded when their parents returned.

We all learned something from those nights that made us a little older and wiser. I thank my friends for their epic parties and the wisdom we gained from those experiences.

Donna Rose

29 | Coming Full Circle

My husband and I both went to Everglades Elementary School in Westchester and originally met in third grade. My parents owned the sporting goods store in the Westchester Mall called ProLand Sports, and every day after school, I'd go to my parents' store and do my homework in the back, and then work with my parents until about 9 p.m. Most of the neighborhood kids bought their school PE uniforms from my parents' store, including my husband, so my dad was kind of an icon and was loved by all the kids. I grew up in that mall!

When I was in my senior year at St. Brendan's High School I went to night school at Coral Park to learn how to be a travel agent, and my dad and I later opened up ProLand Travel in the Westchester Mall.

While I was in high school, my friends and I loved going out to lunch at Arbetter's Hot Dogs on Bird Road. They still have the best chili cheese dogs. Yum! I remember Lila's Restaurant had the best steak covered with fries. The Snack Shack's pizza and the ice cream shop in the mall were awesome too.

My current husband, David Heyman, the man I would marry after meeting again over thirty years later, worked at the pet shop, Publix, Kmart and Linen Supermarket at the Westchester Mall and went to Everglades Elementary School. Although we never dated as kids, he says he wishes he had asked me out back then.

About seven years ago David found me on social media through a mutual friend. We hadn't spoken or seen each other in over thirty years because he lived in Tampa at the time. After about three months of talking to each other every day as friends, he wanted to know if it was weird if he asked me out since we'd gone to Everglades

Gladys Velasco and husband, David Heyman.

Elementary School together. I said it wasn't weird, and the rest is pretty much history. We've been married a little over two years now and he's retired from the Air Force.

Even though the mall is long gone, many of us Westchester Kids still remember the fun times hanging out there. My husband and I created The Everglades Elementary Alumni Group from 1965 to 1985 on social media and we have 157 former classmates on there. A few years ago, we had a reunion at Tropical Park organized by another classmate, and it was a blast catching up with everyone.

Westchester was a great place growing up and we both have many mutual friends from our youth. It's part of what brings us together and part of the special connection we share.

Gladys Velasco

30 | My Buddy

I grew up in the '60s and '70s in Westchester on Twenty-First Street between Eighty-Eighth and Eighty-Ninth Avenue and my neighborhood buddy lived on Twenty-First Terrace just on the other side of my street on the same block, about seven houses around the corner.

He was the friendliest person you'd ever want to meet with a smile as bright as could be. When I was young, I wasn't allowed to cross the street without parental supervision, so it was a great thing that I didn't have to cross any streets to go hang out at his house.

Back in those days, there was very little trouble a couple of youngsters could get into, but we did our best. We used to make little foil rockets and light alcohol to jet propel the rockets. We'd laugh our heads off because he was the one who taught me how to do this, but his grandmother used to scream at me and wave around her broom saying, "Why do you come here and teach my grandson to play with fire?"

Some of my best elementary school memories were eating nacho cheese Doritos and playing Skittle Bowling. One day when we were in fifth grade, we were pranking out at the street in front of my buddy's house. When a car came down the street toward us, one of us would run across the street and we would each squat down low like we were holding a rope across the road to see if we could make the car stop. When the car would stop, we'd laugh and run away.

On one particular day, our fifth grade teacher was the person in the car that stopped as a result of our invisible rope prank. As we were running away, we heard both of our names being screamed by our teacher with the command to stop. Needless to say, we apologized profusely and promised never to do it again. After our teacher left, we laughed and waited for the next car so that we could return to pranking. However, we now knew what car our teacher drove, so we were a little more cautious.

In sixth grade, my buddy had gotten a new bike and had ridden it to school, but unfortunately, his bike disappeared. A day later, while I was on safety patrol, another student from our school pulled up at the corner where I was stationed, and I noticed that he was riding my buddy's bike. I grabbed the bike and held onto it until I could return to school with it so my buddy could get his bike back. We were best friends and it seemed like the universe had delivered his bike to me so I could bring it back to him.

As we got older, we were allowed to take our bikes to Westchester Shopping Center. We'd go to Lionel Playworld to look at toys and sporting equipment and get pizza and a soda.

In junior high school, I remember somebody asking me why I hung out with "that Chinese kid." When I asked who he meant, he identified my buddy. In all those years, it had never occurred to me anybody wouldn't like him just because he was of Asian descent.

In our Westchester neighborhood, we were a big melting pot with families from Cuba, Puerto Rico, Asia, Europe, and some whose roots were firmly planted in the United States.

One of the nice things about growing up in Westchester is that none of this seemed to matter. I asked my buddy about it, and he informed me that he'd been on the receiving end of quite a bit of prejudice. Who knew? He did—my buddy—and it hurt. My friendship with him lasted through high school, but in that time, we'd forged a bond that has transcended the years.

After we graduated from high school, my classmates went their separate ways. Nine years later I was in Tampa, Florida getting my tuxedo for my wedding, and I heard from behind me a few people back, "Hey, buddy!" After all those years, there he was, my buddy. We were able to catch up on our lives and reconnect about our Westchester days. Years later, my wife and I attended his wedding. Our children are different ages, and as it turned out, many friendships were based upon our children's schools and being with the parents of our children's friends.

One day on my way home from St. Petersburg, I was stopped in traffic when my car was rear-ended by another car traveling at a fast speed who didn't notice the traffic flow had stopped. As I was getting my bearings, a voice screamed, "Are you okay?" I knew the voice—it was my buddy. The accident had taken place right in front of where he was working, and he ran out to see if everybody was okay and found me.

In 2016 when my wife and I were doing some last minute shopping prior to moving 3,000 miles away to Oregon, who do we run into at the mall? My buddy! He told us that he and his family were planning a vacation that summer to the great Northwest, and one month after we arrived, I received a text that he and his family would be in Portland visiting.

So here we are in 2021, and the friendship with my childhood buddy is still alive and well. Although we don't see each other as much as in the good old Westchester days, he still has the brightest smile and the friendliest disposition. It doesn't matter where I am, I know that "Hey, buddy" is just a call away—my dear friend and my buddy for life!

Howard Shifke

31 | Neighbors Are Extended Family

Growing up in the Westchester neighborhood of Miami allowed me to have a childhood with fantastic memories. It was the 1960s and that specific neighborhood (Ninety-Fourth Avenue and Twenty-Sixth Street) taught me the meaning of family and friendships. Many of these same people are my friends to this day some fifty-plus years later, having experienced milestone events together, including the births of our children, bar/bat mitzvahs, weddings, and becoming grandparents.

It was a time when neighbors really knew each other and there was no hiding behind a facade. While I've developed many friendships later in life, these Westchester friends really know me. They know my entire family, and what we're made of, where we started, and what we've become.

My favorite memories are walking alone or with my sisters on our block to any neighbor's house and knocking to ask if "so and so" could play. The political correctness of today, where we text to ask if a friend can talk on the phone, didn't exist. If the family didn't want us to play at that time, we simply left and went on to the next house. I miss that for my own kids, who are all grown and on their own. The kids in the neighborhood often walked to school together too.

Robin Ginsberg Paulive (left), 7, dressed as a majorette, with sister Pamela Ginsberg Reuter (right), 9, dressed as a hula dancer for Halloween night in their Westchester neighborhood.

I have a particularly fond memory of when we performed plays, and our mothers supported our efforts. We read library books to decide which story to tell and who would play which role. We rehearsed at each other's houses and set a performance date where all the parents came to watch, and they even handed out bouquets of flowers. We were a neighborhood of lots of girls, so the plays had "girl" roles. I'm not sure I even remember the boys being in our shows as I reminisce now.

My scariest memory was falling off my bike, splitting my chin open and knocking out my front teeth. My sister was the one who ran home to tell our parents I was hurt. I remember my neighborhood girlfriends made me comfort things, like a pillow and some snuggly items to help me feel better while I healed. These are the things I'll never forget.

We also had lots of competitions, like hopscotch, jumping rope and jacks. We spent a lot of time outside and I knew the end of the day was near when around dinner time my mother called my name and clapped her hands. It was time to run back home.

Pamela Ginsberg Reuter

Epilogue ... Last Thoughts
by Jacqueline Gutstein

As I read all the stories from my former classmates and others who lived in and grew up in Westchester, I found a common theme. It was a wholesome era, in a time and neighborhood where families and their kids were happy and felt safe. Just four-square-miles changed the lives of so many Westchester Kids, and their memories live on in their hearts.

Maybe we compare our lives in the present to the one we had growing up in a way that can never be compared. Time has changed the way we live, and technology has catapulted us into a less humane way of communicating, and of socializing. In today's times, we connect with a text or a social media post instead of picking up the phone or sending a handwritten card or letter. I've seen a family of seven sitting at a restaurant, all of them pushing buttons on their mobile phones with their heads tilted down, waiting for their food to arrive. It's almost as if having a face-to-face conversation with your own family is a foreign thought.

Maybe this disconnect is why our Westchester memories are so important to us. We miss running around to our friends' houses and simply knocking on the door to see if your friend can come out and play. We miss seeing our parents walking across the street to their neighbor's house to sit down on the porch or in the Florida room and have some *cafecito* and play dominoes. It was simple back then. We had more patience, more time in a day, and the day seemed to never end.

Westchester wasn't perfect, and it wasn't all good to everyone, but to the majority of the people who lived and grew up in this small neighborhood, it was a good life. A way of life we wish we can duplicate and instill in our children and grandchildren.

I've lost friends and family members during these last fifty years or so, as have most of us, and I've come to appreciate more than ever the sacrifices my parents made and just how fragile life is. "Here today, gone tomorrow" is a saying that has never meant so much to me as when I lost my father and younger brother within eleven months of each other just a few years ago.

Maybe that's why I teared up when I recently got the chance to visit my old Westchester home with my mother, and walk through it, strolling around the backyard where I made so many memories growing up.

The house has been remodeled and the screened Florida room we had, now is enclosed with walls and windows. Gone are the open views to the back yard where a garden once bloomed, where kids ran around playing, giggling, and drinking water from a hose to cool off, where an orange tree gave fresh squeezed orange juice, where birds built their nests on the rose bushes just outside the Florida room, and where a little girl climbed up into a mango tree and thought about life for hours on end.

There is a song by country singer Miranda Lambert titled "The House That Built Me" that brings tears to my eyes every single time I hear it. The lyrics really hit home for me, especially as I arrived at my old childhood home. It tells the story of lady who came back to visit the house she grew up in for one last time, just like I did. The homeowners let my mother and I, total strangers, into their house just like we'd have done some fifty years ago. I'm eternally grateful they opened their home and their hearts to us.

My Westchester house was not just a house, it was my home, and it was my family, my parents, my brothers, and my Abuela Rosa that filled it with love and so many great memories that I will forever treasure. I was truly blessed.

Jacqueline Gutstein

Margarita Gutstein, Jacqueline's mother, at her Westchester home.

Margarita and Miron Gutstein inside their
Westchester home in 1968.

Our beloved Abuela Rosa Kamensky in our
Westchester back yard.

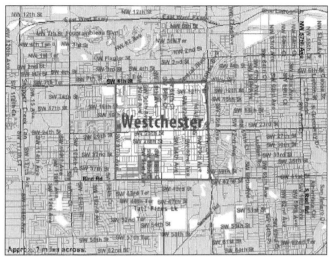

Map: US Census Bureau

The original Westchester neighborhood was comprised of four square miles from the Palmetto Expressway on the east side, west to Ninety-Seventh Avenue SW, north to Eighth Street and south to Bird Road.

As the years went by, the Westchester boundaries increased. Today, Westchester is also referred to as Little Cuba and is no longer in the "middle of nowhere" as some have described it in their stories.

Westchester is now surrounded by many neighborhoods. It is a vibrant community, conveniently located and diverse with many nationalities.

Westchester is also a place that will live on in the hearts and minds of the Westchester Kids.

Made in the USA
Las Vegas, NV
11 September 2021